Elaine's

Elaine's

THE RISE OF ONE OF NEW YORK'S MOST LEGENDARY RESTAURANTS FROM THOSE WHO WERE THERE

AMY PHILLIPS PENN

PREFACE BY LIZ SMITH

Skyhorse Publishing

Skyhorse Publishing books may be purchased in bulk at special discounts for sales promotion, corporate gifts, fund-raising, or educational purposes. Special editions can also be created to specifications. For details, contact the Special Sales Department, Skyhorse Publishing, 307 West 36th Street, 11th Floor, New York, NY 10018 or info@skyhorsepublishing.com.

Skyhorse® and Skyhorse Publishing® are registered trademarks of Skyhorse Publishing, Inc.®, a Delaware corporation.

Visit our website at www.skyhorsepublishing.com.

10 9 8 7 6 5 4 3 2 1

Library of Congress Cataloging-in-Publication Data is available on file.

Cover design by Erin Seaward-Hiatt
Cover photo by Jessica Burstein

Print ISBN: 978-1-63220-272-7
Ebook ISBN: 978-1-63450-007-4

Printed in China

Contents

Preface

LIKE ALL FAMOUS folks who do something really unusual and special in this old world, it's important to understand Elaine Kaufman in a historical context. In the movie *Casablanca*, they say, "Everyone goes to Rick's."

In recent New York, everyone tried to go to Elaine's! Everyone tried to be accepted, tried to get the okay of the owner.

Rick says, famously, "Of all the gin joints in the entire world, you had to walk into mine!"

Elaine said to me when I was writing about her in a book titled *Dishing*: "Liz, don't say I ever threw anyone out; it makes me sound so tough."

Having once been ejected from Elaine's for coming in with a DuPont heiress, which annoyed Don (Donald Ward, Elaine's then-factotum), I was highly amused at this. Don told me that unescorted women weren't welcome; it must have been before Gloria Steinem.

"Unescorted women aren't welcome?" I asked. "I thought they were the best kind."

Elaine found this vastly amusing.

She herself was the original unescorted woman. She never needed an escort, though she certainly liked men more than she liked women.

And men loved Elaine. One of my handsome brothers came to New York just for the purpose of bedding Elaine. So we were more or less "related."

In her time, Elaine's did turn out to be a bit like Rick's. Deals were made . . . controversies spawned.

Dramatic things happened here; here were the beginnings of beautiful friendships and terrible hatreds.

I first met Elaine in the 1950s at Portofino in Greenwich Village. She was then in love with the charming owner, Alfredo Viazzi.

Elaine was a damned good waitress, but she soon bested her Italian lover and became bigger and better known herself, against all odds. Eventually, Elaine's was full of Pulitzer Prize and Nobel Prize winners with a lot of writers eating on the cuff.

She couldn't resist talented people, adored writers, and was the inheritor of traditions from places like that haunt of the old *Herald Tribune* newspaper, Bleeks Artists & Writers Restaurant, where James Thurber would play the Match Game against Lucius Beebe, who was wearing white tie and tails.

In time, Elaine's inherited remarkable literary stars, much like those from the heyday of the old Algonquin Roundtable and from the confines of 21, a place grown glitzy & expensive, as it changed from being a speakeasy after Prohibition. The elite fled to Elaine's, even though the address was inconvenient.

Elaine's was a legend on its own terms, ranking her as a host of the grandeur of John Perona of El Morocco, Sherman Billingsley of the Stork Club, and Toots Shor, who once said of Hamlet, "I bet I'm the only bum here who don't know how this turns out."

Elaine revered the likes of Tim Costello and creative hamburger guys like Danny Levezzo of PJ Clarke's. You couldn't buy a hamburger at Elaine's. She sneered at people who asked for one.

Elaine made up for any lacks. She had stars like Elaine Stritch and Jackie Gleason, who vied for the privilege of serving drinks behind the bar.

She was big-hearted, a closet intellectual in her way, a pushover, but also a hard taskmaster for phonies, fakes, and wannabes—the "civilians," she called the greater public.

She put her stamp on New York café life in an utterly focused career. Though she learned from café & saloon forebearers, there has never been anyone even vaguely like her. Texas Guinan, are you kidding? If Elaine was your friend, you hardly needed a lot of other ones. And in spite of a cynical veneer of sophistication, she was a pussycat, softhearted to a large extent.

Yes, she played favorites and sometimes she could be unreasonable.

One had to mind one's manners in Elaine's. You couldn't be demanding, you couldn't bother and pester the famous, you couldn't ask for autographs.

In 2003, Elaine Kaufman was made a "Living Landmark" by the distinguished New York Landmarks Conservancy.

She was childishly impressed by this honor and she supported this charity, which tries to save New York, ever after, attending every event until her death.

We of the Conservancy were also stunned to discover that Elaine Kaufman's becoming a Living Landmark had sold more tickets and more tables than anyone else except for George Steinbrenner.

While other honorees often accept becoming Living Landmarks—some of them making fun of it all, some bringing others more famous to laud them, and a few singing, dancing, reciting poems or offering films of themselves, and other self-aggrandizements—I shall never get over Elaine's acceptance speech.

I introduced her to giant fanfare, for there was only one Elaine Kaufman and one Elaine's, and her fans were there. She stepped up to the microphone, looked around, and then said simply: "Thank you. I accept this for the late George Plimpton."

It was heaven. It was priceless. It was classy.

It said everything there was to say about art and artists, about culture, taste, good writers, vulgarity, tradition, New York City, indeed, about class, sass, and pizzazz.

—Liz Smith

Introduction

A WRITER'S JOURNEY is an epic one that brakes for "banal." While it's soothing to believe that you have control over your own odyssey, these wise words linger and crescendo: "If you want to make God laugh, tell him your plans."

I am honored and intrigued that Elaine Kaufman and I are reunited in this book.

Elaine's path rose from cosmetician to waitress and ultimately to a restaurateur of colossal fame. Playwright Jack Richardson suggested that Elaine invite writers to her uptown, out of the safe-and-surveyed New York restaurant/tavern turf. He recommended that she use round tables to encourage intimacy and conversation.

Elaine would come to mentor, mother, encourage, and feed her writers.

As I interviewed many of her regulars, the common denominator wrote itself. Many, many regulars and even occasional visitors miss Elaine and Elaine's. They often feel lost, as if their home was uprooted and can never be rebuilt along with its mystique.

My re-entwinement with Elaine's life began on an unassuming day.

One morning I decided to start a Facebook group. I had never ever even considered spearheading an entourage on social media, but there it was: a simple seed spurned my own frustration on what was becoming of the America I knew and deeply cherished.

Reminiscing about all the innovative and magical components that make America "America," I founded a group and named it "Write on America." I invited my ever-sprouting group of Facebook and three-dimensional friends to join me.

My first post was a YouTube of Arlo Guthrie singing "City of New Orleans."

The first seed sunk in, ready to sprout on, be smoked, or blown away. The immediate response came from two "real" friends who remembered the writer of the song, Steve Goodman, strumming his version at J.P.'s, a bar they worked at in the 1970s—not too far a cry from the birth of creativity at Elaine's.

Sasha Tcherevkoff, a Facebook friend who was working for a site named NewYorkNatives.com contacted me. He liked the name of my group and thought that the names might enhance each other or perhaps merge in some way. We made a phone date.

Sasha asked if I was a native New Yorker. I replied that "I was born in Doctor's Hospital."

So began my column, dubbed by NewYorkNatives. com as "Vintage Gossip."

My first column was about Mayor Koch, who had just passed. I had been to Gracie Mansion, met the Mayor, and relished the chance to reminisce in wobbly Yiddish and New York English.

My column grew into a weekly ritual.

I wrote about Elaine's. I told tales of my times there: first as a guest, then a publicist, and ultimately as a columnist and Elaine's occasional lunch companion.

When I received an email from Nicole Frail, an editor at Skyhorse Publishing, my mind was already on my next column, the wild wave that the Surf Club rode. Nicole inquired if I'd be interested in writing a book about Elaine's.

A writer's life is packed and unpacked, the contents scattered almost everywhere but where we discard or carefully fold them. Here I was in California, with a polo pony and three rescue dogs, and I was writing a column for a New York site, and now a book on Elaine's was on the best table that Elaine could offer.

Curiouser and curiouser.

Why was Nicole interested in a book on Elaine's? She replied that it evolved from a discussion that she'd had with her editorial director about New York restaurants in another time. He told her about Elaine's and when he paused, she said, "I wonder if that's a book." A bit of research led her my way. My answer was affirmative: I missed Elaine, and Elaine Kaufman was an intriguing, seemingly complicated, and infinitely controversial woman.

So began the process of researching my subject.

I read every article I could find, A.E. Hotchner's book, *Everyone Comes to Elaine's*, and bartender-turned-journalist Brian McDonald's *Last Call at Elaine's*. Raymond Lindie, who also bartended there, wrote a play titled *Elaine's Paradisio* and a memorable story, "The Beefeater Martini."

I read on: columns and excerpts from Gay Talese, Liz Smith, and *New York Times* editor Peter Khoury, who I consider a new friend in the making. David Black, a screenwriter and the subject of Jessica Burstein's "The Kiss," has also approached that status: potential new friends with treasured memories.

One door opens another—if it doesn't hit you in your bifocals first.

Add on Susan Morse, who contacted Woody Allen for me. To my childlike delight, he actually replied to my questions. Jessica Burstein, Elaine's official photographer, with whom I had worked back in our Studio 54 days, was essential to introducing me to the members of Table 4, which honors Elaine; along with detectives, actors, writers, and assorted other regulars. She has contributed her own funny, loving, vintage Elaine Kaufman diary excerpt, along with several of her excellent photographs.

So many fascinating people entered the doors of this book that I can only beam a seismically never-ending thank-you to everyone I interviewed for this technicolor, touching memory of Elaine's.

I have always missed Elaine's, but now I miss it even more. I wish that I had known Elaine better. The words *loyal friend* are continually chorused in her eulogies.

When you read this book, imagine that we are meeting at Elaine's, in a neighborhood that once was shaky, but shook the trembling and roared into unexpected careers for many into nights that spanned from intellectually intriguing conversations to watching Elaine tossing garbage cans at the paparazzi.

Her inimitable language boisterously beckons asterisks, while her quotes are beyond quotable: who else would dub someone "half a whore"?

Come inside, and share the lore, the inspiration, the tears, and the legend that was Elaine's.

Welcome in.

Photo credit: Susan Hathaway.

So . . . Who Was Elaine Kaufman?

Amy Phillips Penn

OR AS ELAINE might say: Who the fuck was Elaine?

"Yes, I am a fucking icon," proclaimed Elaine Kaufman, the erstwhile, controversial proprietress of New York's celebrity hub, Elaine's.

"Everyone tells me that. What is that? What did you do that is so earth-shattering? Just survive, and you know about that. I guess you get points for surviving," she says in the documentary *I Know a Woman Like That*.

A fucking New York icon she was, remains, and you can put your roulette chip on "the icon goes legendary."

"If you ask me who is Elaine Kaufman, I'd say she's the big mama of them all . . . I'm somebody who is still in the womb, a mother and a motherfucker . . . While I'm waiting to find out how it all turns out, I'll be having a good time," said Elaine.

Elaine Kaufman, Bronx-born, overweight, feisty, and not exactly adored by everyone, soared into the ownership of one of New York's most legendary celebrity restaurants in spite of a prickly stem that should have come with its own app.

Elaine's opened uptown in what was then an "iffy" (think *dangerous*) section of Manhattan, Yorkville, near the corner of Eighty-eighth Street and Second Avenue.

With a New York attitude that could be "abrasive," she kowtowed to no one, no matter how indulgent, celebrated, or powerful they were. Where photographers were concerned, they had to keep their distance and earn her respect—a tough prize to win.

"You're too close to my front door," she screamed at celebrity paparazzi Ron Galella as she hurled a slew of garbage can lids at him. Just one click and an East Side garbage can lid became famous, in a Warhol-esque way.

The woman warrior hurled the garbage top at Galella and hit a parked limousine by mistake. She was not amused. In time, she and Galella put their garbage can lids aside and moved on, though.

"She liked the press I got her," Ron concludes.

Elaine's preference for men was well documented.

"She called men when she wanted fun; she called women when she wanted something," notes Peter Khoury, a *New York Times* editor.

Had this one-time nearly anorexic nighttime cosmologist planned to be the hostess and powerhouse behind one of New York's most seductive celebrity hangouts? Not likely.

Do the math: the restaurant business is one of the best known entrepreneurial gambles, swimming with and against unforeseen tsunamis and fickle clients. Elaine remained relatively calm, cultivated, and rewarded loyalty.

Struggling as a waitress in a restaurant in Greenwich Village, followed by a breakup with its owner, Elaine dug into her very own eponymous digs.

When she built it, they did arrive and imbibe, often running up years of unpaid tabs, and occasionally dishing the dishes: the food at Elaine's was sneered at by those who chose to sneer. But they all came: writers, celebrities, artists, politicians, socialites, athletes, detectives, wannabes, and those she befriended, offered business backing to, hosted weddings for, punched, socked, verbally abused or 86'd.

She has been called everything from a bitch to a hypocrite to a loyal friend.

So . . . how did lightning strike? One tab at a time.

Elaine's opened its doors in Yorkville in 1963. The early sixties were an electrically fascinating time in New York and the world. We lost a president, gained The Beatles, marched against wars, contemplated the life of a hippy, dressed in minis, maxis, and even midis, or emulated Jackie Kennedy.

Writers, singers, and painters had much to explore. Warhol's inundation of repeated images from Marilyn Monroe to the Kennedy assassination entered our collective conscious.

Women were starting to compete with men in the workplace, but were not quite comfortable going solo into a restaurant without a man and making an entrance with a girlfriend was still a bit of an ouch.

Elaine partnered up with Donald Ward to start Elaine's. In a metaphorical coin toss, the name was either going to land on Donald or Elaine. Elaine's it was. The story goes that Donald made his exit after he tried to keep Truman Capote out of Elaine's simply because Capote was gay. Elaine would have none of that, so Elaine's became Elaine's.

As Elaine's grew in popularity, it and its owner were immortalized in song and film. Billy Joel referred to Elaine's in his song "Big Shot" (1978): "they were all impressed with your Halston dress and the people that you knew at Elaine's." Stephin Merritt of The Magnetic Fields mentioned Elaine's in "Love is Like a Bottle of Gin" from the record *69 Love Songs*: "You can find it on the Bowery / Or you can find it at Elaine's / It makes your words more flowery / It makes the sun shine, makes it rain." Woody Allen, who was an Elaine's ultra-regular, featured Elaine's in scenes from his films *Manhattan* (1979) and *Celebrity* (1998). Even the film *Morning Glory* (2010) showed Elaine Kaufman at the bar in Elaine's. The restaurant was also a constant in Stone Barrington novels by Stuart Woods; the first chapter always cites Elaine's as the location of the opening scene.

Elaine's continues to be a subject of conversation many years after its owner's passing. On May 10, 2014, The Moth Radio Hour featured anecdotes about Elaine's. George Plimpton recalled introducing Jerry Spinelli to writers, editors, and director Woody Allen at Elaine's, while José Torres recounted a story he'd shared at Elaine's about his first time facing a white man in the boxing ring.

Alex Gregg and Elaine.

Photo provided by Alex Gregg.

There's No Elaine's Without Elaine*

Amy Phillips Penn

THE FIRST TIME I met Elaine she scared the shit out of me, and I don't scare easily. I'm a New Yorker, after all.

The culture at Elaine's jumpstarted the Studio 54 mentality: Can you get a good table (or in Studio's case, get in at all)? And if you do, can you please get a gander at who's making these decisions?

Michael M. Thomas, who has written many a New York column, found Elaine refreshing. "I got a kick out of her. She was who she was. She learned the art of sucking up to people by insulting them. Elaine was the Toots Shor of the writing world."

Toots was known as "the master of the needle jibe." Take it from there.

---

* This is the article I wrote for New York Natives that caught my publisher's attention. Reprinted here with permission from New York Natives.

Elaine Kaufman was born in New York and was raised in Queens and the Bronx. One of her first jobs was as a night cosmetician. See? Scary.

Ms. Kaufman entered the New York restaurant biz in 1959—no easy odyssey, even back then—when she started running Portofino along with her then boyfriend, Alfredo Viazzi. The artsy crowd gathered and re-gathered: publishers, theatre lovers, writers.

Four years later, Kaufman launched the eponymous Elaine's on East Eighty-eighth Street, where she mothered her chosen tribe: writers. The literati's tabs were known to lengthen and linger. No problem—if Elaine liked you, that is.

Elaine and Norman "don't-fuck-with-me" Mailer dug into a doozy of a drag out that ended with Mailer writing Elaine a letter in which he vowed never to return to her restaurant. Elaine scribbled the word BORING on his pages and mailed them right back to him. A few nights later, Mailer showed up again.

Loyalty doesn't always pay off, but in Elaine's case it did. Vonnegut, Mailer, Plimpton, and Talese were all Elaine's regulars. Woody Allen could usually be seen holding court at his round table. If you sauntered to the loo, you were elbow to elbow with Woody's linguine. How private can you get?

And how did you get to the ladies/men's room? Just ask Elaine. "Take a right at Michael Caine," she might say.

Celebrities celebrated her. Billy Joel immortalized her in the song "Big Shot," and Woody Allen paid homage by shooting a scene of *Manhattan* at Elaine's.

Booking a table at Elaine's was no easy feat. Getting a good table at Elaine's required Herculean-strong connections. And if you weren't going to be in the front room, preferably near a table where Elaine hopped to and from, why even bother? Sitting in "Siberia," does not a New York image make.

Elaine's was center stage for people watching: celebrities, writers, politicians, athletes, and the who's who of the week, whose attendance would surely be noted by *Page Six*.

One torrential night, I went into Elaine's as part of my public relations gig to coordinate a story for a New York news station. I asked Elaine what her priorities were.

"Do what your boss told you to do," she said, and then she ran to Woody's table as if it were on fire to escort him and his guests out so their privacy would remain intact. Her priorities were clear.

How did she treat the press? This from former *New York Post* photographer Adam Scull.

"Elaine was loud, pushy, boisterous, tough-as-nails, took shit from NO ONE, including us photographers. She almost always kept us out on the street cooling our heels whilst the likes of Woody Allen, Robert De Niro, and every other famous actor and author kept coming back for dinner night after night. Elaine's was the place to go mostly because the authors and actors were protected vociferously by Elaine. 'Screw the photographers' I used to hear her say, time and time again, only occasionally allowing just a select few of us in from time to

time. Elaine Kaufman was the doyenne of protective restaurateurs. She caved to no one."

Why did Elaine scare me? Who wants to mess with
that?

In time, Elaine and I warmed up to each other, one
New York edgy step at a time. I had my own column by
then.

"Thanks for the plug," she would say as I walked in.

Elaine slipped into my "like" list surprisingly, but
surely.

When she was going through a slow time, I had a
date with a producer. His secretary called me and told
me that I could pick "any restaurant in town."

"Elaine's," I replied, although the numbers 21 were
adding up in my head.

"You could go anywhere in New York and you picked
Elaine's?" she said.

When we walked in that night, Elaine didn't say
anything, but I knew that she recorded the gesture. We
became friends.

After Elaine's death in 2010, Diane Becker, the heir
to Elaine's, made a decision. Elaine's was closing.

"There's no Elaine's without Elaine," she conceded.

What choice do we have but to agree?

Take Four: Customer, Publicist, Columnist, and "Let's do lunch, Elaine"

Amy Phillips Penn

I ALWAYS LOVED going to Elaine's.

I don't remember the exact date that I went there, but it was sometime in the late 1960s or early 1970s. Glory Days.

I didn't meet Elaine until years later, which was fine with me. She sat with her favorites, changed tables when the mood struck, and had no idea that I was alive. She didn't radiate "warm and fuzzy," and I was happy to keep a respectful distance.

When I first went to Elaine's, it was as someone's "date." Whether it was at Elaine's, 21, aka. the numbers, or Le Club, most of the women took an invisible note as to where they were seated. It was a reflection on their date's allure, not theirs.

There were unspoken rules at Elaine's, such as "please do not feed or interrupt the celebrities," but I was oblivious.

I broke that rule before I knew it was a rule.

On my way out of Elaine's, dressed in a maxi raincoat and floppy brown suede hat, and feeling very *Annie Hall*, I went over to Woody Allen's table and announced that I had a screenplay that I wanted him to see.

I was in my twenties and believed that New York held no barriers especially when it came to writers and artists and lovers of New York like the brilliant Woody Allen.

Artists of all kinds seemed so approachable, then. The art world was booming into pop, op, and anything goes, punched with price tags as bold as a Jackson Pollock.

At museum openings, casual Saturday New York gallery going, art auctions at Sotheby's and parties in the East Hampton, artists and writers mingled with the rest of us, flaunting no attitudes of superiority for the most part. They had all dreamed the dream once.

Woody was extremely gracious.

He told me where to send the script.

"Are you sure that I can't send it to you?"

I was twenty, and felt that you could ask for the moon, and that it just might RSVP favorably. Everyone needs a break, and writers and artists know better than to miss their moment. Embarrassment is a small dividend for having your words published, or echoed on screen.

The screenplay had evolved in my parent's New York kitchen. My mother had painted the walls an electric yellowish orange, which by proxy vote, we had all declared frightening. She and I had visited a famous psychic, who had described the love of my life, who I had (and have) yet to meet.

We decided to write a satirical screenplay about it. The heroine is looking for her prince-to-be, and who could be funnier in that role than Woody Allen? Since he doesn't even know that I exist, the mother and daughter decide to stage a fake kidnapping and leave them on an island for a few days. Naturally they fall in love. The best laid plans . . . But they manage to get kidnapped for real. No one pays the ransom, because they think it's part of the plan. The two lovers are shot. The credits read: "Better Life Next Life" or "The Girl Who Cried Love," on the chalk outlines of their bodies.

Just another New York slice of black humor.

Sometime in the late seventies, I was working for a small publicity firm named Gifford-Wallace. It was run by a husband-and-wife team, Michael (the wife) and her husband, Ed Gifford. They were a small, but powerful team. Their clients had included: *Hair, Godspell,* Studio 54 (from day one), Metromedia TV, and other prime accounts.

My assignment was to go into Elaine's with a Metromedia camera crew and organize a segment on Elaine's. The Giffords had called ahead to Elaine to let her know that we were coming.

It was a torrential night. I arrived drenched, but on time. The camera crew was there.

In my best New York girl school manners, I politely asked Elaine where we should set up. She roared at me, a lioness predator in high hormonal gear.

"Do what your boss told you to do."

No, "please, thank you, or would you like anything to drink?"

What stratosphere was I in and who did you have to cozy up to get out?

Shimmying, in a loose Mumu style dress, this more than ample woman, all but gathered up Woody Allen and a few other customers. Like a mother cat, she was saving her kittens from getting wet by throwing them into the downpour escorted by a chauffeur and waiting limo.

After we finished our assignment, we left without saying goodbye to Elaine. The crew from Metromedia gave me a ride home in their truck. Someone passed around a joint, and soon I was home, the gruff, dismissive woman I had tried to make friends with was soon forgotten.

Sometime in the late seventies and early eighties, I freelanced as an assistant to the world renowned society/ fashion columnist Eugenia Sheppard. I covered parties, movie screenings, younger Manhattan, and pretty much anything I chose that did not conflict with Eugenia's priorities.

When Eugenia died, I was honored to carry on her column with my own byline. I had become a syndicated New York society columnist. I gleaned instant respect, nonstop invitations to everywhere and anything, and a parcel of power, New York style.

I don't know if Elaine and I were ever officially introduced, but I do remember her next words to me after I had written about Elaine's in my column.

"Thanks for the plug," she said when I came in for dinner.

The roar was reserved for elsewhere.

I have arrived.

Elaine feels free to plop someone down at our table. I'm sitting at a table at Elaine's with my friend Patrick Shields.

Patrick was the six-foot-seven director of Le Club, a private dinner club, which hosted Caroline and John Jr. Kennedy's birthday party on the same night.

Jackie O wrote Patrick a handwritten thank-you note. I wouldn't be surprised if he was buried with it.

Can you stand it?

One night, when I was sitting with my friend Harvey Kirk, a publicist for the Giffords and Studio 54, Elaine came over to the table.

John Lennon wants to know if he can get into Studio 54.

"I'll take care of it," said Harvey, and went back to his pasta.

David Black and Barbara Weisberg's wedding. Alec Baldwin is the best man.

Photo provided by David Black.

"Marry Me, Marry Me" At Elaine's

David Black

David Black's awards runneth over, as a journalist, novelist, screenwriter, and producer. Black received the Edgar Allan Poe Writer's Guild Award nomination three times: for best fact crime book Murder at the Met *and "Happily Ever After" and "Carrier" (episodes for Law & Order). Then there's the National Endowment of the Arts Grant in fiction, Playboy's Best Article of the Year Award, and yes, a Pulitzer Prize nomination for* The Plague Years, *and there's so much more. Black has taught writing at Mt. Holyoke College and Harvard. All this, and when he talks about Elaine, he tears up. Black is the vice president of the Executive Committee for the Table 4 Writers Foundation, "continuing the tradition of Elaine Kaufman." We welcome him in.*

THE FIRST TIME I went into Elaine's, it must have been 1968 or something like that. I was writing for one of the underground newspapers and I got an invitation to go to Norman Mailer's birthday party at Elaine's. It was wonderful.

I was a kid from Massachusetts and it was my dream of what every night in New York must have been like—because everyone in New York must have been there.

In 1982 or 1983, I was commuting two days a week from Mount Holyoke, where I was the writer in residence. After my class, I would go directly to Elaine's. I usually sat at the family table with Jack Richardson and we became very close friends. I loved Jack; I actually twelve-stepped him. He was a drinker and a coker, so was I.

That's when I really started going a lot. I met some amazing people and had some crazy times at Elaine's.

There was Bob Datilla, who did all his literary agenting out of Elaine's like it was his office. And I saw Dick Wolf quite a bit. One night, John Henry brought a fire eater into Elaine's and when somebody took out his cigar, she pulled fire from her mouth. Another night, Michael Disend came in with a woman he was dating who was part of a live sex act. She told us all these stories. She had bravado. She said that once on stage she had taken a bowling pin up her ass. Now, Elaine's is usually very noisy, but the room suddenly went silent when she said that.

When I got divorced, I told Pepe, the maitre d', "If I come in here with a date and I look like I'm not having a good time, get me out of here fast."

He said, "What if you look like you're having a good time?"

I replied, "Well, get me out of here faster."

When I met my current wife, Barbara Weisberg, I knew the minute that I saw her—it was like going home—it was love at first sight.

I was going to ask her immediately to marry me. I said, "You're the one. I'm not looking anymore because it's you or no one." I couldn't say it on the first date because I'd cut myself shaving, and if I leaned over, I would bleed all over her. So I waited for the second date and asked her to marry me. She looked deep into my eyes and said. "Are you out of your f'ing mind?"

But she agreed to keep going out with me. It would take me two years to woo her.

For the fourth date, I took her to Elaine's and we kissed. Jessica Burstein was taking pictures that night. Two weeks later, that picture appeared in a *New York Magazine* article about Elaine's.

And over the next years and up until Elaine's closed, Jessica made it a point to photograph our kissing. She's always threatened to put on an exhibit that would show our relationship progressing through seven years by how we're kissing in all these pictures.

When it came time for us to finally get married, we talked to Elaine about our plans. We wanted to have the party and wedding at Elaine's. Elaine turned to Barbara and asked her if this was the first time she'd been married, and Barbara said yes.

Elaine whacked me on the side of the head and said, "What's the matter? Do it right."

So she planned the entire wedding for us, from flowers to a chuppa. And it was a great wedding. We had a rabbi who looked like a leprechaun officiate. Alec Baldwin was my best man and we had a ball.

I love Elaine's and one of the reasons why I—and everyone else—loved her is that when I walked in for the first time, I was an unpublished novelist. A no one with no platform. She talked to me for a few minutes and immediately adopted me.

Elaine didn't much care who you were, where you came from, what your merit badges were. If you were family, you were family. Over the years when I was broke, she'd feed me for nothing. She'd write on my check, "Tip the waiter." As I continued to work, she'd introduce me to people like Marty Bregman and say, "You gotta hire this guy."

When I became successful, she'd do the same thing with me. She'd say to me, "You gotta hire this guy." As I was making more money, I would pay twice as much for my meals at Elaine's to make sure the next guy who was broke was covered.

Elaine paid medical bills, she sent clothes to my home for my kids, and she did that for many, many people— and that was why she was greatly loved.

The best tribute to Elaine is to keep her memory alive, the memory alive of a woman who was extraordinarily special. It matters to many, many of us.

Elaine Empties
the Stanley Cup

Per Bjurman

Per Bjurman became Sweden's leading music writer and was voted The Most Influential Critic by the leading national music industry publication three years in a row. In 2005, he was offered the position as US Correspondent for Aftonbladet, *which he gladly accepted and moved to New York. The following years, he covered everything from elections—not least the historical US presidential election in 2008—to natural disasters, big trials, and space shuttle launches. He is still in New York, working for* Aftonbladet, *but now mostly covers hockey in the NHL, a league in which more than sixty Swedes play.*

I CAME TO New York in January 2005 as the correspondent for the Swedish daily newspaper *Aftonbladet* and immediately decided Elaine's was going to be my home away from home.

I had been there before, when I was just a guest in the city. I loved the atmosphere, the crowd, the exhilaration, and the feeling that anybody could walk through the door at any moment. For almost a year, I dined by myself at the two-person table under a wonderful photograph of JFK and LBJ at Griffith Stadium in Washington, taken by the photographer and Elaine's regular, Neil Leifer.

Eventually, I asked Tony, the great Elaine's waiter, if he would be willing to introduce me to Elaine. "Sure," he said, and walked me over to the Michael Caine's table where Elaine was parked for the moment. Before I even

Per Bjurman and Elaine.

Photo provided by Per Bjurman.

Photo provided by Per Bjurman.

had the chance to tell her who I was, she just growled, "Yeah, yeah . . . you're that Swedish journalist. Sit down."

Nobody came into Elaine's joint that often without Elaine knowing exactly who the hell they were.

From then on, I was part of the family—I always had a seat in "The Line," and, for the next five years, I enjoyed more unforgettable nights under the warm glow of her Art Deco light sconces than most Swedes experience in a lifetime. But it was more than just fun, excitement, and the thrill of having a perfect dry martini placed on the table before I sat down. Elaine became my surrogate mother in New York. She took me in, introduced me to people she knew I would love, and made sure that New York became my new home. It meant everything to me as a shy foreigner, far away from friends and family. There is no way I can repay that kind of life-changing favor, but I did my best in a weekly column I had, and still have, in *Aftonbladet*.

I wrote extensively about the nights on Eighty-eighth Street and Second Avenue. Not so much about the celebrities—though, now and again, I couldn't resist bragging about sitting at tables next to Arnold Schwarzenegger, Robert Altman, Joan Rivers, Larry Hagman, and Richard Dreyfuss—but rather about Elaine herself, her magnificent staff, and the wonderful characters that really were her closest family and also became members of my own New York family: Ash Bennington, Pete Khoury, Helene Gresser, Father Pete, Jessica Burstein, Josh Gaspero, and the incomparable Joey, the unknown Lenny Bruce of the Bronx. After a while, Swedish tourists who read those columns started coming in—and paying for dinner. Elaine really liked that.

Throughout the years, I also brought in a lot of Swedish hockey players. I cover the NHL for my newspaper and have gotten to know my countrymen in the league. Henrik Lundqvist, the New York Rangers superstar goalie, came for dinner a couple of times. We, meaning me and the bartenders Craig and Duffy, both devoted Ranger's fans themselves, made sure Lundqvist got to see the picture of Elaine drinking from the Stanley Cup.

The photo was taken late at night when the 1994 championship team, lead by Mark Messier, came into Elaine's to celebrate, and it hung behind the bar for twenty-five years. Lundqvist looked at the picture quietly for a long time. You'd be excused for thinking that was the moment Henrik Lundqvist decided that he some day was going to win that cup, and drink from it exactly as Elaine had.

Another night, the Detroit Red Wings were in town. A bunch of injured Swedish players, with friends and family, joined me at Ms. Kaufman's saloon. It was one of those magical nights when everyone was hopping tables for hours, while the check somehow followed you around. The night ended at the bar across the street at 4:30 in the morning—with me dancing with one of the Red Wing stars' crutches. That kind of thing could only happen during a night at Elaine's.

When my mother visited me from Sweden, we of course went to Elaine's. My mother doesn't speak much English, but she and Elaine found a way to communicate anyway. At the end of the night, Elaine put one of her big hands on my mother's wrist, smiled and said: "Don't worry, I'll take care of the kid for you."

She sure did. I'm still around and I still love New York, not least thanks to the friends Elaine introduced me to. But it's not the same anymore. Life itself is less exciting without my surrogate mother on the Upper East Side.

I miss her terribly.

"Give Him Table Six, He Says He Has Money."

Steve McPartlin

A former bartender, Steve McPartlin made the fantasy move into reality, as he segued into TV and radio broadcasting. McPartlin was one of the original correspondents for Current Affair, *a host for* Inside Edition, *and a radio sportscaster for ABC Sports.*

IN THE EARLY 1970s, there was a joint on Second Ave up the street from Elaine's named Cavanaugh's. It was run by a great saloon guy named Lou Cavanaugh and his lovely wife Maureen.

I would frequent their establishment often even though I lived and worked tending bar on the north end of the island in Inwood.

One day I get a call from Lou, who told me he hurt his ankle and he needed someone to tend bar. All of his regular bartenders were otherwise indisposed—a fact I would attribute to the fact that there was going to be a severe snowstorm that night. Chomping at the bit to work "downtown," I accepted.

26

It was a slow, slow night and, at about 1:30, Lou said we should leave, so we started to close up with not a soul in sight.

All of a sudden, the door flies open and this two-hundred-and-fifty-pound woman starts screaming and swearing, "Those motherfuckers! What a bunch of fucking thieves!" I looked at Lou, who had a reputation for being a tough guy, and said, "This is all yours, brother." Lou calmed her down and sat her at the bar. It turned out a cab driver wanted twenty bucks for a five-dollar fare to take her home and she was having none of that.

Lou said, "Steve, this is Elaine Kaufman. She owns the joint down the street. Give her a drink." Now, of course I knew who Elaine was because I can read and she was always in the papers in those days. I was studying acting and dating a singer, so I was well aware of the glitterati and literati who frequented her restaurant.

We three had a few drinks and Lou said we were going to drive her home. When we got to her place, I walked her through the snow up to the door and said, "Elaine. I am dating this girl who sings at Joe's Pier 52 and it's her birthday next week. Can I bring her to your restaurant for dinner?"

Elaine looked at me like I was a freak. "Do you have money?"

I said yes.

She replied, "Well, it's open to the fucking public, ya know."

The birthday came and we went to Elaine's. My girlfriend was a bit on the skeptical side that on this, her birthday night, I was taking her to a place where we would be treated like interlopers and placed somewhere near the bathroom and kitchen.

We were greeted by Aldo, a huge guy who had the personality of a Cossack. When I told him I wanted a table for two, he was ready to lead us to Siberia when I spotted Elaine at the end of the bar doing the checks. I said hi and reintroduced myself. She turned to Aldo and said, "Give him table six, he says he has money."

After an hour or so, Elaine sat with us and told us stories and made fun of me treating the place like it was a temple.

We became fast friends and, for the next forty years, I never sat in the back. She always gave me a table up front and she always took care of me.

Not long after that, I gave up the bar for a career in radio and TV sports/news and, whenever I would walk in by myself, she would beckon me to join a group she thought either would be good for me to know or people I could entertain. If you were a journo of any kind, the people she would introduce you to were invaluable, from the famed writers and actors to cops and robbers and assorted members of the clergy.

Anything you ever needed to know about what was going on in New York, you could find out at Elaine's.

The only name dropping I will do: Once I walked in and she grabbed me at the door and said, "Sit with me, I want you to meet Polly Bergen. She likes young guys."

I was fifty at the time so it was a great compliment and I complied.

My last conversation with her was toward the end. It was just the two of us at a table on a Sunday night in the summer. She was lamenting about how business had fallen off. I, trying to put things into perspective, said something to the effect of "Geez, baby, after all these years, does that really matter that much? You own half the block."

My dear friend Elaine looked at me and said in her own very special way, "Hey, asshole, count your own fucking money."

Another lesson learned from my dear friend.

When Elaine Socked Me

China Girard

China Girard is a former Ford model who, along with three other Blue-Blood friends formed The What Four, aka "the first all-girl rock band of the sixties." Columbia Records signed them; they recorded, toured, and were included in an album that boasted two Grammy nominations. Ooh-la-la meets yeah, yeah, yeah. Of course, China went to Elaine's.

In 1966, I was sitting with songwriter Jerry Leiber and *Paris Review* editor George Plimpton, having a conversation about the music business, mostly because I had just started an all-girl rock band called the What Four.

Suddenly a drunk and loud Norman Mailer intruded, demanding Jerry engage in an arm wrestling contest with him. Jerry politely said no thank you and tried to continue eating his spaghetti.

Well, Norman was deaf to the word no, so he plunked himself down in the chair next to me and leaned toward Jerry, grabbing his wrist. Now, I was in the unfortunate position of being in the middle. I scooted back just as Jerry yanked his arm away from Norman's gasp. Then Norman pushed Jerry's hand in his spaghetti, making

Carmen Capalbo, China Girard, and Peter Dinkle.

Photo provided by China Girard.

Jerry furious. George was now on his feet, pleading with Norman to back off, at which point Norman pushed Jerry into the wall. Then hell broke loose. Jerry took a swing at Norman, who kept yelling for Jose Torres to help him.

Jose, being a champion boxer and whose hands were licensed as lethal weapons, could not assist and pretty much backed away, causing Norman to get even angrier.

Meanwhile, I was only feet away at this point when Elaine marched up and socked me in the jaw, thinking that I had started it all. She said, "Men are always fighting over you." Even if that exaggeration was so, it was no reason to punch me. I probably should have punched her back.

By then, the whole bar was in chaos. Norman was escorted out the door by Jose. I took my seat at the table, as did Jerry and George, who said, "Well, that was an interesting episode."

One thing that we could all count on was George's wonderful humor.

How Elaine Became
My Photo Agent

Jessica Burstein

Elaine Kaufman has mingled magic and success into the lives of many. If Elaine was your friend, or simply believed in you, she would introduce you to the world, support you financially, and allow writers to run up unpaid tabs for years. Often, a writer would arrive at Elaine's years, or even decades, later to repay Elaine thousands of dollars in bar and pasta booty. Often, they returned to their lair with Pulitzer Prizes and bestsellers.

Jessica Burstein was a New York photographer who was driving along a challenging—possibly catastrophic—road when Elaine made an emphatic entrance in her life that would change Jessica's destiny.

I KNEW ELAINE Kaufman for a long time before she really got to know me. Although I'd spent time at her restaurant since the mid-seventies, and she knew me well enough to, for example, often try to "pimp me out" to guys whom she thought would like me for my looks, Elaine didn't take me seriously until she saw my photographic work at a gallery exhibition in 1990. It was a defining moment in what would become a rather complicated personal relationship—mother-daughter, friend (and very often foe), and ultimately, the person who became my photo agent.

Somehow Elaine made her way down to Soho, in New York City, for the opening of my exhibition and immediately decided that a triptych of three portraits I'd taken of Truman Capote would look perfect on the wall of "the line" in the front room of her restaurant. She also decided that she'd like to get her paws on another Capote print— this one of him sitting with a stuffed Cobra, which looked as if it were coming out of his groin. In fact, it was Truman's favorite photograph of himself—or at least, that's what he'd told me. Of course, in lieu of money, Elaine offered my gallery dealer the great opportunity to have my work prominently displayed in her restaurant. After she stared him down (and with a little help from me), she got the prints as a gift. Within a day, they were on her walls. Just as quickly, she suddenly viewed me as a woman worthy of her serious attention.

In 1992, during a particularly dry work spell, I was having second thoughts about continuing as a photographer. While in the restaurant, I told Elaine that I was thinking of going to law school.

"Are you nuts?" she yelled at me. "Quit? Kid, you're better than Avedon! You got no place to shoot," she continued, "then come here to do it."

That moment opened to the door for the next twenty years—twenty years of my life I spent as a photographer. Shooting at the restaurant began long before digital photography existed, and so, between the cost of film, processing, paper and printing, shooting at Elaine's was to be the most expensive job I ever had. But it was not without its rewards. In the beginning, no matter what I photographed there, Elaine would have the prints framed and placed on the walls. There was actually a "Jessica Wall," with only my work on it. But it wasn't easy. There were, often, problems dictated by Elaine's moods when she'd decide that I couldn't shoot something that really interested me. That drove me nuts, and we'd get into some heavy fights.

Jessica Burstein with Chris Noth.

Throughout it all, however, Elaine talked me up to anyone and everyone who could possibly give me assignments. Within a year of shooting at the restaurant, she'd introduced me and my work to, among others, television producer Dick Wolf, which resulted in twenty years of work on the *Law & Order* franchise, a published book about the show's crime scenes, and a resulting solo museum exhibition of this work at the famed George Eastman House International Museum of Photography and Film in Rochester, New York. She was also instrumental in getting George Steinbrenner to see my work, which resulted (with the help of the Yankee's President, Randy Levine) in my being commissioned as the fine art photographer for the building of the new Yankee Stadium.

Elaine took every opportunity to try to coach me about how to run business—a subject that has always eluded me. Her efforts failed, because business literally makes me sick. To the end of her life, Elaine tried in every way to get me to understand the importance of business in the arts. She concurred with my father, who'd often told me: "It's not art if it stays in the drawer. The work has to be seen."

After noting, once again, that I was hopeless about business, one of the last things Elaine said to me was "I won't be here, forever. You've *got* to get an agent."

I'm still, admittedly, terrible about business, but one thing that I have made a point of "getting out of the drawer" is my collection of photographs from Elaine's, only made possible because of Elaine Kaufman's unending belief in my talent. I will forever be grateful.

Travels With Elaine

Jessica Burstein

ELAINE LIKED TO travel with me because, frankly, she liked fun and she knew that I'd deliver. Of the various trips we took together, the highlight was our 2005 trip to France.

I preface this story by noting that Elaine was always torn about leaving her restaurant and in particular, as she got older, her trips away became shorter. Generally, she'd last a few days, while endlessly calling the restaurant, and then decide that she needed to go back to Manhattan.

I was planning to go alone, in earlier September, to Vichy, France, when Elaine asked me if I'd accompany her, prior to that time, to the Deauville Film Festival.

Our prep for the trip included:

A. Asking me to push back my planned vacation to Vichy, France, to go with her to the Deauville Film Festival.

B. Speaking with her pulmonary doctor about her ability to travel with breathing problems.

C. Each of us buying a seat in coach (no wild airline expenditure for Elaine and no allowing me my mileage upgrade to Business Class.).

D. My calling the hotel in Deauville at least five times to ensure that her room (not mine), as had been promised, was comp-ed.

E. Calling Hertz to reserve a Citroën, preferably automatic, with enough room for the two of us and . . .

F. For the largest Tumi suitcase, which Elaine had spent days packing.

Day 1:

Three p.m. arrival at JFK, making certain that there's a wheelchair for Elaine. The TSA insists on patting her down. At the time, men were still allowed to do the pat-downs on women. I am outraged. She giggles and says, "Go get me a sandwich." In coach, I'm crushed in the window seat, praying that Elaine has to get up fairly often so that I can move. Every time she does get up for bathroom breaks, I run around the aisles like a lunatic and get back to my seat before she gets back to hers. The flight attendant can't get Elaine's tray table down properly. Elaine tells the flight attendant, "Just rest it on my tits." I stay awake for the full eight-and-a-half hours, while between bathroom breaks and food, Elaine sleeps.

Day 2:

Seven a.m. arrival at Roissy. Check that there's a wheelchair for Elaine. Leave the plane, assuming she'll soon be along. Wait twenty minutes at Customs. No Elaine. Worried, I question every official in sight. Nobody knows anything or seems to care. An hour passes. Frantic, I threaten to sue the airline for losing a passenger. I make up every possible horrible thing that could happen to these people if they don't find Elaine. Another half hour and suddenly . . . Elaine appears, in a wheelchair, a big grin on her face. She tells me that the airline left her in her seat. I ask why she said nothing. Her reply: "You know that I'm shy."

Arrive at Hertz to find that since we are more than two hours late, the Citroën is gone. But, they have one car, a "très belle" stick shift Mini-Cooper (pronounced 'mini-coop-ear' in France) available. I am livid. Elaine insists that we look at it, which we do, since obviously we have no other choice. It's Royal Blue and a convertible and it's love at first sight for Elaine. By some miracle, we fit in—luggage and all. Exhausted, on Paris's *pérephérique*, I get lost for two hours, driving in circles before I figure out the correct "Porte" to Deauville. Elaine is giggling the entire time. I'm going to kill her. Just as I think it's smooth riding all the way to the hotel (for my planned nap), Elaine wants to stop to eat.

At 4 p.m., in a tiny French village, there is no where to eat. I find one small bakery barely open, beg, flash some Euros, and by another miracle, get Elaine a ham sandwich. By the time we get to the hotel, the idea of a nap is a memory, since we are expected at the Film Festival's opening dinner gala and Elaine needs me to unpack for her and help her to get dressed. Our dinner table is filled with men. Elaine's not just in Deauville, she's in heaven.

Days 3–6

Awakened by Elaine's raspy voice on the phone: "You missed breakfast. Havin' lunch?" Seems Elaine is not at all interested in the films at the festival. Her interests included food; reading; the pool; lots of rides in the beloved mini-coop-ear; a visit to the Normandy WWII museum; my translating for her French to English, and vice-versa; endlessly having me call her restaurant to make sure that there are no problems; fiddling with my hair; bragging (to her credit) about a photo of mine prominently displayed in the Festival's catalogue; cocktail parties; dinner parties; and . . . bumping into Roman Polanski. Polanski appears at the hotel's cocktail lounge where Elaine and I are sitting. Having recently won his libel suit against *Vanity Fair* for reporting remarks ostensibly made at Elaine's restaurant, he jubilantly tells Elaine, "I won."

"Big deal," she replies, "You got no real money."

Polanski's reply of "That's not the point," falls on Elaine's deaf ears. I watch, fascinated by how much he wants her approval.

Day 7

Free at last! I'm off, alone, to Vichy. Wait, wait . . . Elaine tells me that she wants to go with me. I can't believe my ears. This woman, who can't normally bear to leave her restaurant, is now extending her trip away from it. She's being insistent and so, I relent. I pack up Elaine's things and my own, and by late afternoon, we stuff ourselves in the mini-coop-ear.

Photo credit: Jessica Burstein.

My plan to drive directly to Vichy, a trip of less than four hours, is suddenly sidetracked when Elaine announces that she wants to fly out of Paris. This means that we have to stay overnight at Orly, because there are no night flights to Clermont-Ferrand. From there, it's an hour's drive to Vichy. Again, I relent. I make reservations for a flight and for the Orly Hilton. The car route to Vichy is virtually a straight line, but going to Orly means a trip back through the dreaded *périphérique* and, sure enough, I get mixed up and find myself coming out of a tunnel onto the Champs-Élysées.

Elaine has been reading and loudly chewing gum throughout the entire ride and only when I mention that

we're somehow on the Champs-Élysées does she bother
to look up. She laughs . . . and laughs. And I'm ready to,
once again, kill her. Instead, I continue on the route to
Orly. It's at this point, when I reach the airport, when the
real trouble rears its head. The route to the Orly Hilton
is designed for travelers coming from the airport itself.
But, if you're coming from outside the airport, it's tricky.
I'd arrived at the airport around 7 p.m. By the time I
found the entrance to the Hilton, it was 10 p.m. Had we
driven from Deauville, straight to Vichy, we would have
been there long ago. Instead, Elaine and I were driving
around for hours and in some really creepy places, and
she thought it was funny. I had to keep the inside light on
while she read, but she met every desperate sigh from me
with a chuckle. Finally, at the Hilton, we each had vodka
to toast what she thought a great adventure.

Day 8

Quelle Journée! Early in the morning, after making certain that our airplane tickets were in order and that a
wheelchair was in place for Elaine to get on the plane,
I returned the mini-coop-ear. I ran back to the airport
gate to find Elaine, expecting to see her in the wheelchair.
Instead, she was sitting on a regular chair. The flight was
boarding and she had no rational explanation as to why
she wasn't in the wheelchair. It turns out that she was
"too shy" to insist on the wheelchair. In consequence, we
missed the flight, at which point Elaine wanted to hire a
car and driver to take us to Vichy. In my head, I added
up what this was costing in terms of money and time.
And I knew that I was putting up with this craziness for

Elaine. I agreed to the car and driver at a fee that was exorbitant—half of which I paid. To make matters worse, throughout the ride, Elaine would repeat, in a mantra-like tone, "Now, *this* is the way to travel!" After what she'd put me through, I was a hair's breadth away from strangling her. Finally, arriving at the hotel in Vichy, we went to the hotel's spa to set up appointments for "Les Soins"—massages, exercise classes, general well-being and "taking the waters." We had an early dinner at which she confessed that she was always worried about money. She said that she didn't really know how to make it, but that she was very clear about saving it. And indeed, she has been very good at that, refusing to exchange her dollars for Euros ("a bother"). When it's necessary to use cash for payment, yours truly remained the banker.

Day 9

Two friends of mine came to the hotel for a pre-planned surprise welcome for Elaine. We called her to the lobby, where they told her that they were inviting her for dinner at the "Elaine's of Vichy"—Brasserie du Casino. Apart from the fact that they knew about Elaine's, she was immediately taken by one of my friends—Bruno Pinard Legry. It was to be the beginning of a beautiful friendship (reference the Vichy bottle, Bogart, and Claude Rains in *Casablanca*). We spent the day at the spa, but for me, the day was spent primarily waiting around to see that Elaine was okay. There were a couple of hitches during Elaine's massages, but none for publication. It was a great night at the Brasserie, where the owner introduced Elaine to the applause of all the patrons.

Day 10

Have to keep my eye on Elaine. In one of the spa's pools, Elaine got into an argument with a Saudi prince over what she called his "harem"—a group of women who were there with him. Got a call in my room, asking me to get over to the spa, ASAP. Arrive to hear Elaine name-calling the prince, who wasn't doing a bad job getting back at her. Both parties use the word *fat*. Hopeless. With help, I get Elaine out of the pool. Later, she tells me that she's proud that she stood up for women—the irony of that remark escaping someone who is, in fact, known for being mean to them. I say nothing. But, in the meantime, I speak to the prince, having already met his beefy, gangster-ish bodyguards. I tell him she was sorry to have offended him. At the concierge's desk, a gift from the prince—a Burberry scarf is left for me. I give it to Elaine, who immediately throws it in the garbage. Things improve that night as Bruno takes Elaine on a solo "date" at the Brasserie, the "Elaine's of Vichy."

Day 11

I'm tired. I love Elaine, but it's a lot of work taking care of her. I haven't had a real vacation in three years and I need Elaine to leave. Don't know how to ask her. We take a cab ride through the city because she's unable to walk it and I want her to see as much as possible. Turns out that I don't have to ask her when she's leaving. She tells me that she has to get back to the restaurant, that this is the longest trip she has ever taken and plans to leave tomorrow. I spend the afternoon interviewing drivers because I want her to leave happy. This means finding a young, handsome, and charming male driver to take her on the three-hour drive to the airport, with food stops adding time along the way. I find him. Tonight, we go for a farewell dinner at the Brasserie, the only restaurant where Elaine wants to be.

Day 12
Ten a.m. Elaine meets her driver. She's ready to dump me in half a second and get going with Mr. Young, Handsome, and Charming. Bruno and friends come to say goodbye. I'm oddly feeling a little separation anxiety, as are my friends. Elaine is a major presence and something will be lost with her departure. We stand on the street, feeling small, waving like little children to a parent saying goodbye. Tonight, we will go to the Brasserie to toast her with all the patrons, who've become "family" at the "Elaine's of Vichy."

Addendum—Two weeks later:
I arrive at Elaine's and people virtually bow down to me. Elaine calls me over and says, "Thank you. I've told everyone that this was the best trip I've had in my life." She's the kindest that she has ever been to me. I'm not hungry and she's not making me eat! Unheard of! It feels way too uncomfortably weird, but I needn't have worried, because . . .

The following night:
Elaine is back to being the not so "shy" Elaine of her restaurant. There, I'm immediately greeted with the growl: "You betta be havin' dinna!"

Candace Bushnell, Gay Talese (behind), John Scribner, Jr. (at her foot), and Richard Behar (with cigar) celebrate the Oscars.

Photo credit: Jessica Burstein.

My Last Night At Elaine's

Jodi Garner

*Jodi Garner is the author of "The 45-Year Old Intern"
published in* The 52 Weeks *by Karen Amster-Young and Pam
Godwin (Skyhorse Publishing 2014). Jodi is also the producer
of* The Smart Kids Guide to Grownups, *Off-Broadway, in
production; associate producer,* Disaster! A 70s Disaster
Movie Musical, *Broadway, in production; associate producer,*
The Jazz Singer, *Off-Broadway, in production; producer*
Danny Boy, *2005 New York Fringe Festival Audience Favorite;
and associate producer, Stephen Schwartz's* Captain Louie,
*Off-Broadway. Jodi is also a board member of The W. Eugene
Smith Memorial Fund for Humanistic Photography. Jodi lives
in New York City with her fourteen-year-old twins and was at
Elaine's on the last night before it closed in May 2011.*

B, R, AND our friend A, who had also joined us many a
night at Elaine's from 2004 through the end, and all of
whom always stayed way later than me, were on hand for
the last night at Elaine's. B made all the arrangements for
us to get in that night and she, R, and A got there early.
I had to get the babysitter settled so I arrived later. By
the time I got there, a crowd had gathered, the likes of

which I hadn't before seen in front of Elaine's. TV crews and cameras were on hand to document this momentous occasion. While there was a festive air in Elaine's that night, a tribute to when Elaine's was Elaine's, there was also a sadness. Elaine's was a refuge; a community. For the regulars, holdovers from the go-go years, and the more recent additions like myself when almost anyone could get a table along the wall, there was almost a nervous merriment. What would happen to us all when Elaine's was gone? Where would we all go to be connected, to be a part of the community?

I wasn't particularly sad that last night. Elaine and Elaine's had come into my life for a season and a reason. Elaine's was there when I needed it and Elaine Kaufman was Elaine's.

Without Elaine, there just couldn't be anymore Elaine's.

"I'm a Fucking Icon."

Elaine Madsen

"You have to interview me. I'm a fucking icon," Elaine announced to Emmy Award–winning director Elaine Madsen while Madsen was working out the details for her film I Know a Woman Like That *(in which Elaine Kaufman's interview appears). The film has been recognized by the Rhode Island International Film Festival with their "Helping Hand International Humanitarian Award," given annually to a film that inspires social change, community outreach, and a better understanding of the world in which we live. When the film screened at the Chicago International Film Festival, Roger Ebert cited it as "transformative and extraordinary."*

ELAINE HAD NO varnish. That's what I remember most about her. Within minutes of her sitting next to us, the greeting turned into a conversation about something— something you cared to talk about. I am not famous, I brought nothing to the table but myself; her famousness never sat down with her.

She found out I was a writer and asked to see my book which I didn't have with me.

When I came again, she asked after it right away. She really wanted to see it!

Elaine Madsen interviews Elaine Kaufman.

Photo credit: T. J. Rosza.

When my daughter, Virginia, told Elaine I was doing a documentary, which Virginia was producing, Elaine immediately said: "You have to interview me, I'm a fucking icon!"

And she grandly repeated that memorable quote for the interview. She knew we had no big sponsors, no big budget and for sure she knew she was doing far more good for our story than any good we could conceivably bring to her.

In our interview, she spoke to me about her childhood
and her voracious reading habit—a childhood character-
istic we shared. When the interview concluded we shared
a glass of wine and she suggested it would be good for
our film if I captured a night at Elaine's. I wouldn't have
asked. But, shortly thereafter, I got a call and an invitation to let us film her forty-fifth birthday party; for certain a highlight of the film.

We were very happily surprised that our cameraman
was the only one filming the event.

Shortly thereafter, my daughters and I came to
Elaine's to celebrate my birthday. She surprised me with
the most elaborate birthday cake I'd ever seen and a
beautiful rose. As Diane set the cake in front of me, she
whispered in my ear, "She doesn't do this, you know."

Did all of us have moments with Elaine that she
"doesn't do"? That was one of ours.

Celebrating Elaine Madsen's
birthday at Elaine's with her
daughters. L to R: Virginia
Madsen,   Elaine   Madsen,
Cheri Borowiec.

Photo credit T. J. Rosza.

Elaine Was
My Dating Coach

Ken Pliska

Ken Pliska moved to New York City from Scranton, Pennsylvania in 1987. A graduate of Pennsylvania State University with a degree in architectural engineering, his early career was in the architecture and engineering field. In 2000, he started working in real estate development and consulting as an owner's representative. Currently, he is partners in the firm Second River Station, LLC. His wife of eighteen years, Kimberly McGovern Pliska, passed away in 2008.

Ken made many friends at Elaine's, from celebrities to the average local. He hung at the bar but also sat at tables. Because he was a middle-of-the-road kind of guy, he was able to start the "All the People that You Knew at Elaine's" Facebook page and was invited to be on the board of the Table 4 Writers Foundation.

Elaine's was a saloon he called home. It was a place that helped him heal during the most difficult period of his life. Elaine once informed him that he was "a slab of meat on a hook." And so began her work as his dating coach.

My FIRST STOP in Elaine's was in 1987. I had just moved to NYC and was checking out restaurants and bars on Second Avenue. I knew nothing about Elaine or the place, but it looked fun and I popped in. I had a few drinks but it wasn't near my apartment, so I didn't make it back for a few years.

My wife and I moved to the Yorkville neighborhood in 1992. Elaine's became our local spot for a special dinner. Since we were not regulars, we typically got seated in the rear of the restaurant. As the years passed, we went from one to two visits a year to about eight to ten. This was still not regular status, but Elaine knew our faces, as this went on for more than ten years.

In the fall of 2008, my wife had an accident and passed away. My dear friend, Joni Loeffler, was a regular who had been going to Elaine's for decades. Joni insisted that I spend more time in Elaine's. She said, "It will help you heal."

I found myself in Elaine's about four to five nights a week. Shortly after this change to my schedule, Elaine took notice and asked Gianni, the head waiter, "What's the big guy's story?" Gianni filled her in and she asked me to join her and tell my story. From that moment, Elaine and I were friends.

I did heal in Elaine's. I met many new friends and Elaine was always on the lookout for the proper business and social connections. She was a master of the art of networking. After about a year, she also became my dating coach.

It was December 2009. I was sitting at the bar on a quiet evening. After Elaine came in and got settled, she joined me at the bar. In the middle of our conversation, she stopped and asked, "Are you ready yet?" I had no idea what she was talking about.

I said, "Ready for what?"

Elaine replied, "Are you ready to start dating again?"

I said "Sure, I guess so."

Her response was, "Good, because you're a slab of meat on a hook." I guess this was an Elaine-styled compliment.

While I was a late part of the Elaine's family, the last few years of the restaurant meant the world to me. I will forever miss the comfort of her saloon.

My Home
Away From Home

Dana Moyles

Dana N. Moyles has been in the commercial real estate industry since 1993. She has worked in both NYC and Chicago. She has represented owners, landlords, and tenants. She has worked as an Asset Manager and Leasing Agent. She currently runs her own company and is focusing on Tenant Representation in NYC and Chicago. Clients include Chicago Cut Steakhouse, The Local Chicago, Bobby Van's, Cibo, NIF Services of New York and Satori Investment Partners. Ms. Moyles graduated from Lehigh University in 1994 and is highly active in the alumni community. She is a licensed real estate broker in New York and Illinois.

How DO I explain the impact and the history Elaine's has had in my life? I am not famous or literary; I am just a woman who works hard in her life for her career, family, and friends. So this is a tribute from someone who was lucky to find Elaine's and have it become part of her world.

From the first moment I stepped in the door in my evening gown at twenty-four, to my last drink there a couple of years ago, it had been my home away from home, my safe place to go. I grew up at Elaine's.

And I was blessed to become someone who can be called a regular even after I moved to Chicago.

There are so many memories. Duffy, the bartender, wanting my keys! Birthdays celebrated for me and my father. Elections won and lost (thanks to Alex, the other bartender, for being my ally). Sporting events survived! Being the lone Mets fan in the Subway World Series—it was Elaine who protected me from being harassed.

Boys dated and dumped (thanks Duffy to for saving me from the Hand!). And one tragically lost on September 11. Through that loss and the immediate aftermath, I vividly recalling sitting outside crying and Duffy rescuing me. And always taking care to make sure I was okay.

Through my father's illnesses and my mother's death, Elaine's was the safe place to go. There were people to support me and always a hug from a wonderful woman who granted me her kindness. I am so lucky.

And, of course, all the friendships started over the years. The bar people and table people. How that's all become part of my history. People who have become part of the fabric of my life especially Rosemary, Tommy, Duffy, Alex, Ray, Malcolm, Frank, and Johnny (sorry the lottery numbers never panned out, Johnny). And the other friends who were in from out of town and became friends like Rich Cooper.

I loved knowing Elaine was so happy for me when I moved and that she embraced me when I came home every time. She encouraged me, told me I looked beautiful and happy. And she always knew that if I was in NYC, I was coming to see her. We made deals about my future. I am grateful that she knew and liked John. She met the man I love who even my mother never got to meet.

And then there were the best New Year's Eves ever. With Rosemary, Chris, Kathleen, Fraser, Traci, Darci, Kurt, and John, to name a few. What can ever compare? Certainly not New Year's Eve in Chicago.

These are just some of my memories. I cry as I write this, knowing I wasn't there for the final night. But I post and send this in honor of the woman and the legacy of Elaine Kaufman. Bricks and mortar may change hands but the impact of you personally on my life can never be altered.

The Good Penny

Curt Block

Curt Block couldn't resist contacting me with this role-reversal story. His date, after trying to make nice to Elaine with dismissive responses, finally told Elaine to "fuck off." Tables were turned, and none were in Siberia.

Curt Block worked for twenty-four years in the NBC Press and Publicity Department in New York with responsibility for entertainment, news, and sports. Block also spent five years as a sportswriter at United Press International and worked on many other impressive media accounts.

He's not quite sure if he visited Elaine's after this night.

MOST OF MY earliest visits to Elaine's were with Jessica Burstein, a close friend for many years. I had been introduced to Elaine several times but never had the feeling that I'd had made any lasting impression on her—or, in truth, *any* impression.

One night, in the late 1990s, I visited the restaurant, sans Jessica, with a stunning young woman named Penny. She was aware of the restaurant, but had never been there. To my surprise, our meal was better than any other than I'd had at Elaine's. Truly unexpected.

Preparing to leave, I asked my date if she would like an after-dinner drink at the bar. It was relatively early so there was plenty of room there.

I suddenly noticed Elaine seated alone at a table directly opposite the bar and whispered to Penny that I thought I should say hello to the proprietor. I approached the table to ask if I could join her. She gave me a quick once over and said: "Suit yourself"—clearly not a warm greeting, but still, not a rejection, which I'd often seen with so many others who'd approached her.

Having twice tried to compliment Elaine, Penny had received no reaction or eye contact and she looked at me as if to say "Get me out of here." Within a minute, however, she'd had enough, turned to Elaine, and in a voice loud enough for anyone in the restaurant to clearly hear, said: "Fuck this!" and bolted from the table.

Having more invested in Penny than Elaine, I quickly paid the bar bill and looked for Penny, who was by this time already outside, on Second Avenue, flagging a cab.

This story has stayed with me, because knowing how intimidated most people were of her over the years, I've wondered how many customers' actual last words to Elaine were to "fuck off."

Ash Bennington and Elaine.

Photo credit Alex Rass.

"Elaine's Was Really Three Different Places."

Ash Bennington

Elaine's was not only "three different places," but it could easily be described as three different times. Ash Bennington was there for the final chapters.

Ash Bennington is a former CNBC reporter with fifteen years of financial services experience. His work has appeared in the Christian Science Monitor, *TheStreet.com,* BusinessInsider, ZeroHedge, *and numerous other publications. He is currently senior editor at Roubini's Edge, a subsidiary of the economics consultancy Roubini Global Economics.*

PEOPLE OFTEN TALK about Elaine's during the glory days—in the sixties, seventies, and eighties—but Elaine's was magnificent until the moment Elaine died. I started going to the restaurant regularly around 2006, about five years before it closed. Elaine, and Elaine's, changed my life in ways I still don't understand. When I started going to Elaine's, I was working in banking, but wanted very much to be a writer. Somehow, Elaine's made that possible. I got my first two writing jobs standing at the bar, though I still don't really know how it happened.

Elaine's was an insomniac's paradise. Elaine knew that writers lead solitary lives, and that they crave comradeship at night. (There's a lot of overlap between the categories of "writer" and "insomniac.") I was at the restaurant perhaps four or five nights a week, usually after midnight. There were other kinds of people at Elaine's besides writers and reporters—show business people, Wall Street types, FBI agents—but they all loved the nighttime.

Late at night, the lighting at Elaine's was an oasis. Warm light is no small matter for refugees from sleep. I once mentioned this unusual quality to one of the regulars, and was told that Elaine had bought the fixtures from a funeral home.

The first night I attempted to go to Elaine's by myself, also late at night, I didn't make it through the front door. There was a writer standing in front of the restaurant— a writer I had studied years earlier in college—with a blonde woman on one arm and a brunette on the other—smoking a cigarette. I was so nervous that instead of going into Elaine's I had dinner at the Midnight Express Diner next door.

Yes, there were movie stars too. Elaine's was closed four days a year: Christmas, New Year's Day, Fourth of July, and Oscar night, when she threw the *Entertainment Weekly* party. One night, someone snapped a picture of Arnold Schwarzenegger on their iPhone. When Schwarzenegger came over to kiss Elaine goodnight, I showed the photo to him. Schwarzenegger said in his dense Teutonic accent, "You should put it up on the Twitter."

The celebrities at Elaine's were like fine art hanging on a wall: They were always around—and every once in awhile you remembered their presence with awe—but then you returned to the conversation at hand. Elaine's was about conversation—with other regulars, with the staff, and, of course, with Elaine herself—all blown together through her door by the night wind.

Another night, I saw Peter O'Toole come in for dinner with the legendary publicist Bobby Zarem. Walking across the terra cotta tiles, in the electric glow of the funeral lights, O'Toole cut no less an impressive figure than he had walking across the Al-Nefud desert in Bedouin robes.

"Table hopping," floating from one group to another, was the norm at Elaine's. Groups dissolved and merged over the course of nights that often did not end until nearly dawn. For my thirty-fifth birthday party at Elaine's, I invited some friends I used to work with at a bank. One of the guys from the IT department tapped me on the shoulder and said, "Is that Jack Nicholson at your birthday party?"

I looked up and saw Nicholson, talking with someone I'd met at Elaine's a few months earlier. Of course, Jack Nicholson wasn't at my birthday party—but, owing to the odd nature of Elaine's, he wasn't quite not at my birthday party, either.

"To tell you the truth, I'm not sure," I said.

That was the way Elaine's was.

If there was a secret to Elaine's, other than the magnetism of its proprietress, it was that Elaine's was really three different places.

While the restaurant got most of the attention, the bar was a great New York saloon. The bar fed the restaurant new blood, and kept it from acquiring the claustrophobic feel of a private club. The fact that anyone could walk in off the street for a drink at the bar always kept the game interesting.

The side room of the restaurant, called Siberia by the regulars and staff, ran on reservations. It was the kind of room where a group of businessmen from, say, Chicago could come for a veal chop, a martini, and a healthy dose of New York night life while they were in town.

But when most people talk about Elaine's they are referring to The Line—where the table hopping happened. The Line was the row of round tables along the wall where the regulars, and Elaine herself, held court. In the course of a good night, a regular might sit at six or eight different tables, joining and rejoining groups for hours on end. It was a phenomenon I have not seen before or since. (Side note: Whenever one of the customers from Siberia asked, "What's the best table?" Elaine replied, invariably, "The one I'm sitting at.")

The Line is where the writers sat. One night, I joined a party of four at a table with Elaine. After a few drinks, I leaned close to Elaine and said "We are the only two people at this table who don't have Pulitzer Prizes." Elaine just shook her head; to her, they were simply two old friends.

The night Kurt Vonnegut died, I saw Peter Khoury, an editor at the *New York Times*, as I was walking to my table. Peter said to me, "Kurt Vonnegut has just left us."

Before his meaning became clear, I turned toward the window to look for the great novelist—whom I mistakenly assumed had just left the restaurant. As the night drew on, a number of other writers arrived. They, too, it seemed, felt sorrow at the loss of a legend—and were somehow drawn to gather among their compatriots at Elaine's.

Of all the conversations I had with writers at Elaine's, the one that stands out most in my memory lasted barely fifteen words. I'd been introduced to Gay Talese that night, and the person introducing us had told Talese that I was working on a novel. Talese shook my hand and said "Finish it." I nodded and said "Yes." Gay pumped my arm slowly, stared into my eyes, and said, "No. Finish it. Do you understand? Finish It." I believe I replied, "Yes, Mr. Talese." His analysis was spot on—but, since his advice went unheeded, I'm still a little anxious about meeting him again.

But what I miss most is having dinner alone with Elaine. The honor of eating dinner with Elaine alone meant that the house rules of conversation would be suspended. There was no need to fill the air with words. It was like sitting inside the eye of a hurricane, as everything around you spun. Eventually, you'd be swept up into the whirlwind of the night.

Woody Allen and Elaine.

Photo credit Ron Galella.

Woody Allen On Elaine's

No story about Elaine's would be complete without Woody Allen. Many, many thanks to Susan Morse, an outstanding film editor, who collaborated with Woody Allen for many years, for the connection.

Do you think that Elaine's personified New York?
At the time, Elaine's did not necessarily personify New York to me, but in retrospect it seems like a good question.

What was your most memorable time at Elaine's?
My most memorable time is almost eating there every night for ten years.

Any great romantic moments at Elaine's?
Nothing particularly romantic occurred and no single funny incident although I had a million laughs there in dinner conversations with friends.

If Elaine was cast in a movie, who do you think should play her?
Kathy Bates is one person who could play Elaine.

What drew you to Elaine's?

Elaine's was like a club. One great thing about Elaine's was that while there was a lot of action going on all around one had complete privacy at one's table because everyone there was so famous that there was no celebrity ogling, no autographs asked for and it was quite a private dinner. I simply ate, enjoyed looking around, and rarely socialized but was always friendly if anyone said hello. I never ever wore a hat at Elaine's. Also I shot several scenes at Elaine's and not just *Manhattan*. It was in *Manhattan Murder History* as well and *Celebrity* and maybe even more that I am forgetting.

Top Ten Reasons Your New Hangout Will Never Replace Elaine's

Charles Kipps

Charles Kipps has won Emmy, Peabody, and Edgar Awards and is the author of several books. Kipps' TV scripts include Law & Order *and* Colombo. *He has written and produced music for Gladys Knight, Aretha Franklin, and the Temptations. Impressed?*

Charles Kipps wrote a Top Ten List of "Things I Have Heard Elaine Say" for A.E. Hotchner's book, Everyone Comes to Elaine's.

Here's his custom-made Top Ten List for us.

10. They close down if there's a blizzard.
9. For some reason, the tables in the bar are considered undesirable.
8. If you haven't been there for a few days they don't make you feel guilty.
7. You can mention other restaurants and not be thrown out.

6. The owner doesn't sit with you and eat off your plate.

5. If you stop in after attending an event that included dinner, they don't make you order food.

4. It's okay to send back an entrée if there's something wrong with it.

3. The patrons all seem disturbingly normal.

2. You can go home whenever you want.

1. There will never be another Elaine.

Warner Leroy and Elaine once discussed diets at an event.

Photo provided by Bridget Leroy.

Shooting Elaine's (But Not Elaine)

Ron Galella

Ron Galella is the paparazzo who pursued and then pursued some more. Galella doesn't "do" no, especially from Jackie O. Elaine threw garbage cans at him; Marlon Brando allegedly punched him in the jaw. Galella has been in and out of courtrooms, defending his right to click on. He is the subject of Smash his Camera *and the author of* Jackie: My Obsession.

DURING MY "GOLDEN years" of shooting—in the 1960s and 1970s—when there were freedom and opportunity, I covered Elaine's Restaurant. Elaine's was a late-night hangout for celebrities, especially writers, and was, of course, Woody Allen's favorite. I usually made it my last stop of the night on my way home to Westchester. One of my many great takes was on September 14, 1978, when I photographed Woody Allen and Caroline Kennedy. Not together, of course, but each out with friends. That night Woody did something unusual: he decided to walk home going west on Eighty-eighth Street. I was behind him, with his back facing me, and I yelled to him,

"On the count of three, turn around." I counted, and to my surprise, he actually turned around! That photo was used for an artist's rendering, which was published on the cover of the April 30, 1979, issue of *Time* magazine. I was paid the cover fee, $750!

Woody and Mia Farrow had a hot new romance at the time, so my wife Betty and I waited to catch them leaving Elaine's one night. Unfortunately, they ran out separately to Woody's Rolls Royce, but Betty and I surprised them shortly thereafter at a traffic light on Central Park West. They tried to dodge the cameras by hiding in the backseat, but we were able to catch them by each shooting through the back windows. Betty actually wound up getting the better shot, and those were the first photos of them together!

When Spinelli
Met Plimpton

An Elaine's Legend
As told to Amy Phillips Penn

GEORGE PLIMPTON, THE legendary editor who competed in sporting events, acting, and comedy in Las Vegas, all for the power of a hands-on, pen's-on story, was a regular at Elaine's.

One tale that has been told and retold and, like a good game of "operator," invites literary salt and paprika, was the night when Jerry Spinelli, an aspiring writer-to-be, found his way to Elaine's via George Plimpton. Jerry's wife, Eileen, had all but decimated their savings to buy an auction promise of "A Night with George Plimpton."

And so it was off to Elaine's.

"Table after table was filled with literary bigwigs: Kurt Vonnegut, Jill Krementz, Irwin Shaw, Peter Stone, Dan Jenkins," Plimpton recalled in Hotchner's *Everyone Comes to Elaine's*. At Elaine's, though, it was understood by all that you never, ever interrupt Woody Allen.

However, Plimpton dared to brave it in the name of the up-and-coming Spinelli.

"Woody," he said, "forgive me. This is Jerry Spinelli, the writer from Philadelphia."

"Yes," Allen said evenly. "I know."

While Spinelli embraces the memory of his one and only night at Elaine's, he says that the Woody Allen introduction never happened . . .

To date, Jerry Spinelli has published close to thirty books, both for children and adults. He recounts the story of his night at Elaine's often at lectures, and in less formal settings.

"George Plimpton contacted me before he published a magazine article on our night at Elaine's. He suggested that he might embellish a bit. The Woody Allen story is the only embellishment I remember, as it simply did not happen."

What did happen was a cab ride to remember after dinner at Elaine's.

"It was not long after our night at Elaine's with George Plimpton that I had my first novel accepted for publication by Little, Brown. I can't say there was a direct link between the two events, but this is for sure: a recounting of that night has entertained audiences I've spoken to for more than three decades.

"We left Elaine's that night in a taxi. The cab first dropped Plimpton off at his place. We said our goodbyes and headed for the train station to return home. As we were stopped at a traffic light, the driver turned to us and said, "I couldn't help overhearing your conversation. Are you writers?"

"Yes," they replied.

"Well—" he said, and he reached down to the front seat and when his hand reappeared it was holding a stack of paper that looked familiar: a manuscript. "I happen to have a book of my own here," he said. "I wonder if you would mind having a look at it."

"We had to tell him we were not qualified to do so—not yet, anyway—but his heartfelt request brought the evening around to a perfect circle. The reason Eileen had bid our life savings in the first place for a Night on the Town with George Plimpton was to give my manuscript an audience with a famous writer, trusting that publication would surely follow."

"Not Only Did You Share A Meal Or A Drink, But You Shared Yourself."

Mark Rossini

Mark T. Rossini became an FBI Special Agent in July 1991, and after new agent training at Quantico, Virginia, he reported to the New York field office. Mr. Rossini worked on complex white-collar crime cases for the first six years of his career, concentrating mostly in the areas of public corruption, financial fraud, and corporate malfeasance. Years later, Mr. Rossini extensively traveled on sensitive counterterrorism operations, working with foreign law enforcement and intelligence agencies.

Mr. Rossini has lectured at the FBI Academy, the CIA University, and many government and private institutions regarding the PATRIOT ACT, FISA, and the operational duties and responsibilities of the FBI, CIA, and the NCT.

I FIRST STARTED going to Elaine's around 1995. I became an FBI agent in 1991 and worked mostly in Manhattan and The Bronx. I had always heard of Elaine's, having grown up in New York, and having an apartment just a few blocks away from its fabled location, but I was too busy with something or another and never had an opportunity to go in. I started to go there regularly with my boss John P. O'Neill after he transferred in from FBIHQ. I have to say it was an amazing place. The mixture of personalities and professions was incomparable. From the Police Commissioner to the titans of Hollywood and finance, Elaine's was the place where everyone gathered and "shared." Not only did you share a meal or a drink, but you shared yourself. You were able to cross those visible and invisible lines that separate classes and professions, in an atmosphere that essentially was a private club managed by an indomitable presence and personality. Elaine was the power and force at the center, and you better heed to her instructions and advice on anything and everything. From her menu suggestions to telling someone (and I mean anyone no matter who they were) to sit with you and talk if she thought it would do either one of you good. We all dutifully listened like children. Many of us referred to her as Mamma. I would call another habitué, Steve Levy, on the phone and say, "See you at Mamma's tonight." We never said "Elaine's."

I think that's what hurt most about her passing. It was like losing your mother. Elaine's was like your home, and you were always welcome. Sunday's were referred to as "family night." After I would see my parents up in Westchester County, I would stop there and have some quiet time with the rest of the "family." I remember one Sunday night that changed my life. My mom had a stroke on September 11, 2000 (one year before the event that changed our lives). After her stroke, she deteriorated to the point where she was in a wheelchair and becoming atrophied.

In the fall of 2004, I was having a family night meal with Elaine and Dr. Richie Saitta, another loyal and faithful habitué, and Elaine asked me how my mom was doing. I put my head down and said that she was in a very bad state and that we were looking for homes to put her in. Dr. Richie asked after condition and I told him the story. Without hesitation, he said, "She has to see Michael." Michael being Dr. Michael Kaplitt, MD, another loyal patron and the number 2 of neurology at New York Hospital Weill Cornell Medical Center.

Dr. Richie called Michael right there, and the road to my mom's miracle recovery started. Turns out my mom was misdiagnosed with Parkinson's. What she had actually was hydrocephalus or "water on the brain" as a result of the emergency craniotomy that was done on the night of the stroke, which all other doctors failed to see except Michael. After he operated on her, she walked out of the hospital and continued to walk and walk and walk . . . up to nine miles a day until she died recently of cancer.

My other boss in the FBI was John Miller, who is now the Deputy Police Commissioner for Intelligence at the NYPD. John was fond of saying that there "wasn't anything that couldn't be solved or fixed at Elaine's." And he was right.

Elaine's, A Tribute

Photographs by Larry Fink

Dabney Coleman Does *The Godfather* Gig At Elaine's. Just Guess Who's Listening.

Dabney Coleman

Dabney Coleman is an actor who can make you laugh even on a long-distance phone call. He came to Elaine's via his role in Tootsie; *most of the crew ate, partied, and revived themselves at Elaine's, along with the film's director Sydney Pollack. Pollack donated a piano to Elaine's: Dabney Coleman did duets with and without the piano. Among Dabney's sixty-plus roles, he is remembered for his villainous take of the sexist/ tyrant boss in* 9 to 5. *Gotta love him.*

THE FIRST TIME that I went to Elaine's was when I was in *Tootsie*. I'd never heard of the place. Somehow a whole group of us decided on it; Dustin (Hoffman), Jessica (Lange), I don't know whether Geena Davis was there or not. That was the first time I heard of it. Elaine was very cordial. It was a very celebrity-oriented place, a hot place forty years ago and it remained hotter.

Woody Allen was there virtually every night, it was a fun place. I mean politicians, cops, bad guys, mafia guys, athletes, writers, press people, hot lawyers, and other restaurateurs.

The way that Elaine set it up was quite unique. She was a very large woman, a very powerful woman. If your table wasn't ready, she'd grab somebody and say, "Norman Mailer, this is Dabney Coleman, you guys talk to each other and your table will be ready in a minute."

Sometimes you might talk for a minute or two, and sometimes you might stay right there, where she put you, and consider yourself to be very lucky to be talking to Norman Mailer, or the Mayor of New York, Ed Koch.

You never knew what the luck of the draw would be and that was the magic of it. And she would add to it from time to time by coming over and joining you. She was a fun person, knew what great combinations were, and was a great catalyst. Paul Hornung was there, the golden boy of football, so you might sit with him, which I did for an hour or half, or right next to Ralph Connor, homerun champion in the 1940s or 1950s, or guys like Joe Pepitone, Cal Rifkin, or some gangster.

Elaine had said of one such person, "Well, he's going to jail tomorrow for fifteen years, this is his goodbye party."

These firemen were there, maybe eight of them at a long table, and I saluted them when I knew who they were. They were from Firehouse 10, which is a pretty notorious firehouse; they lost almost everybody on 9/11.

Sydney Pollack was a great aficionado; of course Woody Allen. I went in with Louise Lasser a couple of times, and Gianni Uzielli who had his own restaurant, Uzi's. He's gone unfortunately, but we became very good friends.

You just would see this very rich combination of people at Elaine's. One night, I'm looking over at this large table, obviously all Mafia with one bodyguard and one guy with his arm folded, keeping track of who's coming in the door. I started doing my Godfather impersonation. They can't hear me, but they can see me and it was very clear who I was doing.

The bodyguard watches me for a few minutes, deadpan in the beginning, and slowly this look crept across his face and he can barely contain himself. He whispers in this guy's ear, and the guy turns around and looks at me and he hits the guy next to him and it goes all the way down the table and they're leaning over motionless and soundless.

So, now I raise my voice a little bit and know I've got them. Some of them had this noncommittal grin and some of them did not. They were all riveted. But not necessarily smiling at the end, I gave this backhanded wave, and said "Buona Sera" and they all applauded. Stuff like that would just happen at Elaine's.

Do you know the song "Why, oh why, oh why, oh, did I ever leave Ohio?" I'm one of the few people who can do the harmony to it. It's a very pretty, sweet little song.

One night at Elaine's, I catch Edie Adams, who was in the show it came from. I stopped Edie and said: "Excuse me, what if I told you that I knew the harmony to 'Why oh why oh?' How'd you like to sing it with me?"

So we tuned it up and we started singing this song. The whole place went dead-ass silent.

We get a standing ovation.

And lo and behold if it wasn't in Page Six in the *New York Post* the next day.

Photo provided by Susan Hathaway.

Elaine Kaufman:
Friend and Investor

Esther Margolis

Elaine was Esther's first investor, and unsolicited, at that. So began Esther Margolis's phenomenal company: Newmarket Publishing and Communications, and Newmarket Press. An ingenious publicist of the literary world and their books at Bantam, Margolis worked with Maya Angelou, Gore Vidal, Gail Sheehy, and other illustrious writers. Her dazzling creative know-how was key to the global success of the Guinness Book of World Records.

I GO BACK with Elaine to the late sixties, a long time—1966 or 1967, when it was really becoming known as a hangout for authors and journalists. I was at Bantam books, as head of publicity and marketing there.

One of the men I worked with suggested that we go to Elaine's. It was uptown at Germantown, and I didn't know anyone there.

I started going more frequently in the late 1960s and early 1970s, because I knew a lot of journalists and I had been friends with a few men at the *New York Times* and one of the few women, Lacey Fosburgh, who worked at the *Times*.

She happened to be quite a gorgeous girl. She was related to the Whitney family, which was only important in that it gave her access to people. (After she left the *New York Times*, she covered the Patty Hearst Symbionese Liberation Army and was one of the few journalists privileged to interview the reclusive J. D. Salinger.)

Lacey was quite terrific and amazing. That's who I knew, and Sidney Zion, David Halberstam, Gay Talese, Warren Hinckle, and that whole crowd.

That was fantastic for me, because I was doing publicity at a paperback publishing house. I'd only been in New York for six or seven years and it was exciting for me, because there was a lot going on the sixties, and Elaine's became my dining room.

Elaine's would go on till four in the morning. There were backgammon games and gambling. I was single, I was free, and I would go down there till late and still make a meeting at Bantam at 7:30 in the morning.

During the making of the film *Tootsie*, which Sydney Pollack was making in New York, I was doing the book of *The Making of Tootsie*. My first two film-related books were *Tootsie* and *Gandhi*. That was in my first year.

They gave me full access to the *Tootsie* set. Pollack would do the dailies at night and come into Elaine's after; he was at Elaine's practically every night. He wound up giving Elaine a piano as a gift after *Tootsie*.

Elaine's was wonderful, wonderful experience for me.

There was a time when I wasn't going there as often as I had been. I was reluctant to go there as a woman on my own, as much because I was on my own as because I was a woman and it was the seventies.

If I had a business lunch with a male, I would get to whichever restaurant early and have them run the credit card to make sure that the check was taken care of. It was clear that men at that time were embarrassed if women were picking up the check. Elaine's didn't take credit cards at that time, though, which made this trick difficult.

I would often see Elaine at publishing parties. When Elaine saw me at these various functions, she made a point of asking why I wasn't coming in.

"Well, you know, I'm not seeing so and so anymore."

She said, "No, you come; I'm setting up a house account for you."

From that point on, I was more comfortable going there and taking men for business dinners.

People were surprised that I was so comfortable. I invited Nora Ephron for dinner there one night and she was somewhat taken aback.

She said, "The two of us?" and I said sure. I'm sure it was the first time Nora was there with another woman.

It got easier as I got older, and people were more accustomed to seeing women in the professional world. I went there a lot as Bantam was growing as a company. It wasn't a place that you had to put on airs and obviously it was interesting. Elaine was very good at maintaining your privacy, often suggesting that you might want to meet someone, as she also maintained contacts. She would whisper in my ear, "So and so is over there and has a new book. Would you like to meet him?"

One time when Woody Allen was sitting with Mia Farrow, I was sitting opposite them. Elaine came over and said, "Do you know who is over there?" Looking at a table of two women, one I knew, a journalist, but the other one I didn't recognize.

She said, "That's Simone de Beauvoir."

I said, "Oh, really?"

Woody Allen actually got up and walked over to her table to meet her, which he apparently never ever did. And they conversed for several minutes. The woman with Simone waved me over and I went and talked to them for ten or fifteen minutes. It was an exciting moment.

Elaine had high regard for me, which was wonderful, and she became a really good friend. Socially, when I would date anyone seriously, I would take them to Elaine's and she would make a point of coming over. She had a way of assessing people and, within three minutes, she would whisper in my ear something either good or bad. The first time that I took my late husband Stan to Elaine's, she came and sat with us about five minutes, leaned over, and said: "Keep this one."

We were married for over thirty years.

We had a regular table at Elaine's.

There was a time that Elaine tried to build up a lunch trade in the 1980s that didn't work.

Stan worked nearby and he would come in and have lunch with her. He was a psychologist who had a specialty in self-hypnosis.

There were certain courtesies that you would maintain at Elaine's. I would call to say I was coming and make sure it was okay. I recognized most of the waiters' voices.

Elaine followed my career. I was at Bantam until 1980. When the Agnelli group had basically bought Bantam, I took a few of the Italian group there and they loved it and made it their regular spot before they sold the company.

When I decided that I would be leaving Bantam, Elaine was very encouraging that I start something on my own. I wanted to have an equity-based company in publishing and consulting.

One night, Elaine put something in my hand. It was a check for a considerable amount. She said, "Whatever you do with it, kid, I know you're going to do it right. Here: Figure it out."

I hadn't even gone out to raise any money yet, so she was my first investor.

Her early reputation was that she didn't like women, or that she only gave her attention to the men who came through the door, but that wasn't true. She had a lot of women friends: Rona Jaffe came in and Carol Higgins Clark was a regular.

Elaine was really good at respecting your privacy, if that was what was really called for. I came in one time for a business dinner, and the maitre'd, I think it was Elio, said that he was so glad that I was here and asked who I was meeting. He never asked that kind of question, so I asked why and he said, "Because I have to see who to place at that table back there. . . . I have to be careful who I put back there, that's why I'm asking you."

I said, "Well, who's there?"

He whispered, "Elizabeth Taylor."

I said, "You can put me back there; I'll be good, I promise."

I made sure that my chair was facing hers; I wasn't going to give up that moment. She was lovely. She was there with two bodyguards. It was between her marriages to Burton, she was single at the time, and she was gorgeous. They had to stop me from following her into the ladies room. I'm exaggerating, but it was tempting, I have to say.

Elaine's was that kind of place where they were concerned that people were not bothered.

Elaine was knocked a lot for the food there, but you just had to know what to order. You didn't go there for the food, anyway.

"I Was Married To My Restaurant; Elaine Was Married To Elaine's."

Steve (Pally) McFadden

Steve McFadden partnered up in 1979 to launch New York's famous McFadden's restaurant on Forty-second Street and Second Avenue. His customers included Daily News *reporters, U.N. dignitaries, and those who simply loved to party. Then it was on to Elaine's.*

ELAINE WAS A very good pal of mine. I went in there when I was a young kid just out of school and it first opened, then I didn't go again for a while. I have a place called McFadden's on Forty-second and Second that opened in 1979.

In those days, we had all the press people and people like that McAlary, Drury and Andrew Cuomo. We would all hang out at McFadden's and then we would all go up to Elaine's and close the joint. It wasn't every night, but it was on a fairly consistent basis, and that's how I

96

became a pal of hers and that was how she became a real good pal of mine.

She did a lot of good things for a lot of good people. She was gruff in her demeanor, but strong when it came to taking care of her people.

When she opened up, she may have been one of the first women to own a restaurant or saloon. She found a very strange location, when she opened up in 1963. In those days, it was all men, usually three or four buddies who went to school together. She was a pioneer in that respect, ahead of her time; she was like the ultimate feminist. She was as tough as any bar owner in New York City, getting exactly what she wanted in terms of the décor and the clientele.

She was totally hands on.

She did it very well for a very long time, she had boatloads of friends, but they loved her tough demeanor. If she had been a sweet little lady, they wouldn't have enjoyed the place. And it was like when she said something rude to you; it was almost like a badge of honor. *Yes! Elaine yelled at me.* Get out of that seat and move over.

One time Geraldo (Rivera) was in there. This guy—I think his name was Michael—he was a reporter for *Newsday*, I believe, was in there. Out of the blue, this creep, this bozo, Geraldo started picking on him. This guy's a little guy and Geraldo was an ex-boxer in his day. Elaine interceded. A lot of f-bombs were thrown and out the door went Geraldo.

The next day she says to me, "Pally, do you believe this thing?"

It was a big wreath of yellow roses, and looked liked a mobster's funeral piece, from Geraldo, saying he was sorry, that sort of thing. I don't think he ever came in again. It didn't matter.

It would have been easy to take his side of the thing because he was a celebrity. Elaine could have stuck up for the celebrity, but she stuck up for who was in the right, she wasn't worried about who was better known: that was sort of like the integrity part of her. That's why Geraldo apologized with the flowers and I guess he felt like a jerk.

Elaine wasn't really petty about things, she'd say what was on her mind. It was part of a day's work. People can be an idiot one day and the next day they apologize and you forget about it. I've been in the saloon biz for more than forty years. If someone acts up one, you forget about it. That's the way life is, people have a few drinks, and even without drinks, this one isn't talking to that one.

Elaine had her favorites; they were people who interested her. If someone spent a lot of money, she wasn't upset about it by any means, but she was more interested in their conversation and what they brought to the table than what family they came from.

The Elaine's saga is a really noble one, believe me. She really ran things. She loved to laugh, she loved to have fun, and she loved to come into her place every night. If she had a cold, it would drive her crazy to stay in. She'd be calling the place five or six times a night— who's coming? Who's leaving? Sometimes, she even came in at eleven if she was sick. She would be there *every* night. It was her place. She took a few days off to go to the Deauville Film Festival; and she closed only two days a year on Thanksgiving and Christmas. She never stayed home, though. She would go to P.J. Clarke's.

She could be a girlie girl when she wanted to be. She was very complex.

I had a cancer operation. I was in Sloan and I get this thing of flowers and it's from Elaine's. People asked if I knew her. So I go, yes, she's a pal of mine. I went home after three or four days, and I got a delivery of flowers and with it was a container of chicken soup—and it was *hot*, that was the thing. She'd call and say, "Did you have the fucking soup? You feeling better now?"

When she got older, she really loved when young people would come in and when people would bring their sons and daughters. She wanted to stay young all her life. She thought young, and as life went on, she lost a lot of close friends. Elaine was a person who looked at tomorrow; that's the secret of aging.

Then it was her time. An awful lot of laughter went out of the placed just like that.

You could say about Elaine, like the line from *The Last Hurrah*, "How do you thank a woman for a million laughs?"

She provided that. People miss her to this day. There'll never be another place like that in New York. We're lucky we caught it.

Elaine Was An Interesting, Tough Lady. (I Saw Her Punch Out A Guy.)

Ken Moran

Ken Moran started out on the lobster shift at the New York Post, where he talked a woman out of committing suicide on the phone. Moran became a sportswriter for the New York Post, and celebrated his first front page, which had little to do with fun and games, at Elaine's.

THERE WERE DIFFERENT groups at Elaine's, but we were the second generation. The first generation was 1960s and early 1970s, Gay Talese and all those people.

But then Elaine's had a down period. We—myself, John Miller, Michael McAlary, and a whole bunch of newspaper media people—started her up again in the mid 1980s. We kind of revived the bar energy and what was going on there.

It was just a great playground.

Elaine was an interesting, tough lady. (I saw her punch out a guy.)

I got close to the bartenders, especially Tommy Carney, and I got to meet a lot of great people including Joey Heatherton, who jumped on me the first time we met. I looked at her and said, "I don't know who you think I am, but I'm not him."

She had thought I was Derek Sanderson, who played a lot of great hockey for the Rangers. Apparently, I looked like him. And as it turned out, later on that evening she was sitting by herself, and I sat down by her and I ended up dating her for about a year.

There was a famous night when I was in there with Paul Hornung and Keith Hernandez. The three of us were the only ones in the place aside from Tommy and some models, and Paul was so drunk that he fell right off the barstool three times. This is a guy who won the Super Bowl three times. We had to pick him up and put him back in the stool. I was amazed at how many times he did this. Most of us would have been dead.

At Elaine's, I was always amazed at who I would run into in the men's room. For the most part we were all very friendly, like Arnold Schwarzenegger and what's his name—Rambo (Stallone). All of a sudden you'd be in the middle of a conversation with people in the middle of doing your business. It became quite natural after a while.

Everybody had a book party at Elaine's. The most poignant one for me was Mike McAlary, a columnist for the *Daily News*. He had a number of his book parties there. He was about as good a friend as I had. His last book party was right after he was diagnosed with cancer, and everyone showed up in the newspaper business because they realized how sick he was. I was in tears. He wrote some great stuff in a book that he gave me. I had to keep walking away, so he wouldn't see me in tears.

After fifteen years of that place, I'm lucky I'm still here. I love the fact that Elaine would sit down and talk to you and always try to help you with your career and push you for better things.

I was a sportswriter, but there was a time I was upstate and there was a murder in the Catskills, and I was up there, playing golf. So, I get a call from the desk and I covered the story. It was the first time I ever had the front page. On my way home, I stopped in at Elaine's, and she had all these people there and I got a standing ovation.

I became one of her boys, and she threw birthday parties for me a couple of times. I would always have one of the prime tables up front and people would look at me like, *Who the hell are you?*

Erica Jong, Stuart Woods, and Elaine.

Photo credit: Harry Benson.

The Era Is Over

Al Sapienza

Al Sapienza is well-known for his roles in The Sopranos *and* House of Cards. *Betwixt and between, he sang Beatles duets at Elaine's. He is the over-the-moon father of a little girl who is affectionately known as Lambchop.*

I WAS ON tour with Beatlemania in 1977 till around 1980. I would go to Elaine's now and then. When I got *The Sopranos,* I started going to Elaine's once a week.

I'm a real wanderer and traveler. I work between New York, L.A., and Toronto and I always go to dinner by myself. You could go into Elaine's by yourself. She kept several tables for herself and her friends, regulars and celebrities. I'd sit at one of those tables and have these incredible conversations with people who had interesting jobs and an incredible influence on our culture.

I'd have a political conversation with a guy from *60 Minutes,* and three days later I'd be sitting with a Broadway actress, and then I'd be talking to Ray Kelly (the former police commissioner) about law enforcement.

Once I brought a friend, a CEO of an airline, to Elaine's. I ordered a steak and saved that part near the tip for the end. Then Elaine leaned over my plate, cut it off, and ate it with her fingers before I could.

That same night, my friend says to her, "What you are doing for the holidays?"

And she said, "What the hell you think I'm doing? I'm going to be here. I'm working."

I met a bunch of women there. Elaine was a major matchmaker for me. But when I was ready to get married and have a child, I looked elsewhere. I didn't need to meet the mother of my child at a restaurant bar.

I actually went on the Internet to find a wife. I wanted to meet someone outside my entertainment world, someone much more grounded than myself. I met the perfect person; she's a psychiatrist at Mount Sinai—Dr. Michelle Widlitz. Elaine liked her the second she met her; she looked at me like "you're a smart guy."

Anytime that I'd go to Elaine's with Michelle, Elaine would sit at our table for at least a half hour and we'd have these great conversations about everything: politics, Bloomberg, and whatever else was going on.

Elaine would always offer us a round of drinks when we were ready to leave and didn't want to eat or drink anymore; never in the beginning when we were going to drink them.

When we decided to get married, I had my bachelor's party and my rehearsal dinner at Elaine's. My wedding was at the Essex House. I invited Elaine to come out of respect, but I didn't think she'd show. I really wanted her to come, though. And she did.

For the centennial, I sang at Elaine's with Uncle Junior, my partner in *The Sopranos*. We sang a bunch of Beatles songs on New Year's Eve in 1999. It was the greatest place on Earth as far as I'm concerned.

When that place closed, that stopped. I was friends with Fred Gallo, who designed practically every Broadway set, and other Elaine's regulars. I'm too busy to call those guys and they're too busy to call me. There's no place anymore where everyone goes. The era is over.

Every time I walked in, either Josh (Gasparo), Dr. Joe, or Tony Danza would be there to sit with. There's no restaurant in New York like that. It's just over. The era is over.

Photo credit: Walter Bernard.

Still "Anchored"
At Elaine's

Bob Drury

In the mega macho days of reporting, Bob Drury personified the game. Drury began as a copy boy, then a sportswriter, then crime reporter and eventually as an editor of a well-groomed men's magazine. He is the author/co-author editor of nine books.

ELAINE'S WAS AN anchor. It always was; it was the place I would go.

Elaine's served so many purposes. When I was a police reporter for *New York Newsday* in the mid 1980s, if I needed to get something out of a detective, I would take them to Elaine's. This was in the middle of the crack wars.

I would call Elaine's and I said "the usual." I'd come in and she'd make a big deal out of whomever I was with and offer us a front table. I'd say, "Elaine, do you mind? Can you hold that table for us? I'd like to go in the back and talk to Detective Shapiro here."

Of course, his eyes were all sparkling because she had made such a big deal over us. This had been all planned. We'd go in the back and talk for a few hours and then she'd put us in the front. I swear, it worked like a charm with every homicide detective I ever interviewed. This was pre-planned.

She liked me.

We went back to the early eighties. I had a literary agent, Jay Acton. He had an old Yankee ballplayer, Ryne Duren, and Ryne was an obstreperous type. People knew him as "the man with the coke bottle glasses." He was blind and half drunk when he played and everyone knew it. His warm-up pitches were a hundred miles an hour. He never knew where they were going.

He'd gotten sober and he'd gotten God. So Jay said, "Listen." (And I was a kid, I think I was a sports columnist for the *New York Post*.) "Could you go live with this guy for a month in Minnesota and polish his book? I've got most of it."

I did. Anyway, the book comes out eight months later. Jay calls me and says he has a check for twenty-two grand, something that made my eyes bulge at the time. Jay said, "Why don't you come up? We're having a book party at Elaine's tomorrow, before she opens."

Elaine's! At this point, I'd never been to Elaine's.

So I go there, and there's Jay standing at the door and he pulls out the check. I knew no one there. Tommy was at the bar. I asked for a Bud. I took out some money and he said, "It's a book party, pal. Don't you know anything?" I left a two-dollar tip on the bar.

This went on for a few hours. I didn't know anyone there, so I just kept drinking.

I noticed that there was this kind of daunting woman sitting at the bar and she was kind of watching me. I said, "Hi, I'm Drury, I'm one of Jays clients."

She said, "I know who you are. I saw the size of the check you got. I've been watching you give two-dollar tips to the bartender every time he gives you free drinks. You're fucking welcome in here."

I said, "Who are you?"

She said, "I'm fucking Elaine."

It was the beginning of a beautiful relation.

When she hit that time in the late 1980s when celebs weren't really coming in any more, things were emptying out, and I think the newspaper guys, especially those who covered cops, really kind of buoyed her.

When she got hot again in the 1990s with the celebs, she never forgot me, Esposito, McAlary, and Moran. She always had a special place for us, because we maybe bridged a hollow period for her.

Everyone used to compare Elaine to Toots Shor with that whole irascible thing. Was that an act? I don't think so. I think she was pretty irascible, but she was also loyal. She was like a mean old junkyard dog, but once you got her on your side, she was loyal. I can't think of another place that had such a strong female owner. She knew her stuff about journalism; she treated the early *SNL* guys as her own. I'd heard that men had fucked her over in her life, but once you had given her loyalty, she gave it right back. She was really mean to women, she was jealous of women, especially pretty women.

Like it or leave it, she liked me; I used to be a big handsome strappy guy. I don't have a clubhouse in the city any more, and that was our clubhouse.

I entered it one toe at a time.

She was always good to me.

"Who's Da Poet?"

Taki Theodoracopulos

The last conversation I had with Taki was about having "fuck-you money." We were at a party in some New York townhouse. Perhaps it was his.

Taki's column High Life *has been in* The Spectator *since1977. In 1984, Taki took time out from all the glam and did penance in Pentonville Prison for possession of cocaine. In 2002, he founded* The American Conservative Magazine *with Pat Buchanan and Scott McConnell. Yes, he's controversial, from racial slurs to his own "fuck-you money," but never, ever boring.*

THERE WAS ALWAYS a place for me because she made a special compensation for drunk writers or journalists. She always had a good table for me.

I always had editorial meetings on Sunday nights at Elaine's. I had a section called Taki's Top Drawer in the *New York Press*. So we used to meet, five, six seven of us to make the plans for the week's issue right there at Elaine's.

She used to join us and put in her two cents—more than two cents, the whole dollar, mostly. She used to tell us who the good guys were, who the bad guys were . . . It was fun to have editorial meetings there. She used to advertise and never pay us. She ever took something off the enormous bill. It was a unique to have the meetings there because people were actually inspired.

I started going there in the 1960s and early 1970s along with Norman Mailer and Nigel Dempster. When Clay Felker brought myself, Anthony Haden-Guest, and Nigel Dempster over from England, the place to meet up was Elaine's. There was always a good table, especially for me, because unlike the rest of the British hacks, I paid my own way.

I think that the only time that she got angry at me was the time that I came up from the Village. There were these two guys outside just begging for money, and I brought them in for a drink (I was drunk). And she just lost her temper.

"Never do that again."

One funny incident that I remember: there was a very *Romeo and Juliet* note that I send to girls so I quickly wrote that thing on *Spectator* paper, the magazine that I worked for, and sent it to a nearby table of girls and guys. I was sitting with Elaine, by the way, because she used to come and plunk herself down. And after about ten minutes, this wonderful actor who I had never seen before, Joe Pesci, he came up and said, in a very loud voice, "Who's da poet?"

So we all looked around and said, "What you are talking about?" and tried to dismiss him. Then he whips the note I'd written to the girls.

"Who said this?" he asked.

I said, "I did."

He said, "Listen, kid. I wouldn't do this if I were you. Those guys are all gangsters."

I remember Elaine saying, "Nice going, kid."

She was always very funny because nothing would ever shock her.

Elaine with director Roman Polanski.

Photo credit: Jessica Burstein.

Elaine As Mama Earth

Fred Morton

Frederic Morton has contributed columns to the New York Times, Esquire, *and* Playboy. *He is the author of several books including* The Rothschilds: Portrait of a Dynasty. *Not too shabby for the son of a blacksmith. The Austrian-born Jewish–American writer immigrated to America in 1940 and started his career as a baker before studying literature. Watch him go Freudian.*

WHAT I LIKE about Elaine's is that it was a home away from home; it had the same appeal that it had to most of its habitués, and that was all Elaine's personality. She was not a restaurateur, she was a den mother.

If she'd had children, the restaurant would not have been nearly as attractive. If you went there three, four, or five times, and you weren't utterly personally repellent, you became one of her children, which meant that she started yelling at you instead of being polite.

If you were doing something that displeased her or she thought was bad for you, she was yelling at you. The people of course were all in show business or media places where you feel on one hand you were part of the

A gathering for Dr. Joe Platania's birthday at Elaine's.

Photo provided by Susan Hathaway.

glamour group, on the other, these people were all loners, including, me. You want Mama, no matter how old you are or how successful you are, and she was Mama, and part of the Mama is the yelling, at least if you were brought up in a Jewish family as I was.

It's very strange. I think her size contributed to it, that enormous body that suggested Mother Earth, that she was capable of having an infinite number of children. The ducklings kept circling around the mother duck. If you didn't come back that week or at least the week after, that was a betrayal and that betrayal, once she voiced it, it upset me, but somehow after the initial upset, there's a warmth after. "She missed me, I mean my God, she missed me."

She conveyed to you that you were not the restaurants' customer, but that you were a beloved child. That was more important than the food, which was not as bad as it was reported to be. I'm lucky because I have such an obtuse palette that it didn't make too much difference. The restaurant looked sort of sloppy and messy, and you felt that you didn't have to dress up. It was like home. At home you could throw away your tie and come as you are, which is basically naked and sloppy—not naked in the literal sense.

The downside of all this was the ego confrontations among those who were the well-knowns and those who wanted to be known. All that was complicated by the overall warmth once you were part of her brood—and that included people who were not well-known. She was just as human and vain as all of us. She liked the idea that she had all these names in her heyday, which lasted a long time, but basically it was the idea of having a family evening.

She once told me it was expensive for her. It's not nearly as expensive as Le Cirque or other expensive restaurants, the average time which people spend at a meal there is two hours. At Elaine's, the experience lasts four hours or more because people start table hopping. And even if they order more drinks, it doesn't make up for the loss of turnover. "But it means financially a loss for me, and the worse thing is that I like it that way. Because it means they love being here," she said.

"In a blood sense, I don't have a family, but what are you going to do if you're in a family? I have it here. There are really terrific people to talk to every night. I prefer my Elaine's family because a family is always loaded with problems, which is really boring. There has never been a night there when I've been bored. Not with the people who come to Elaine's." (Everyone Comes to Elaine's, Hotchner.)

There's "Nothing Like Gedempte Flaische."

Steve Walter

Steve Walter is an owner of the Cutting Room, a live music venue, restaurant, and bar since 1999. He graduated from Berklee College of Music, played in bands, and taught guitar in New Jersey. Versatile in style, he was a woman's coat manufacturer for more than a decade. And the beat rocks on.

AFTER THE FIRST time I went into Elaine's, I became addicted. You met so many nice people there and Elaine would never let you be alone. It was like the old school.

I've met so many incredible people there. If she could help you in any way, she'd call and say "Tell Stevie to come down."

If she thought she could introduce you to someone romantically, she would. If you ate with Elaine, she'd stick her fork into what you were eating. But you had to eat, she didn't want a saloon. She'd rather you ate fifty dollars' worth of food than drink one hundred dollars' of liquor. She'd say "nothing like gedempte flaische," which is Yiddish for potted meat.

She was sharp as could be and always knew what was going on in every inch in that place. She was there, always making sure that you were having a good time and never alone. If there was no one for you to eat with, she'd eat with you. She had great stories.

She was a class act all the way, if she liked you. You know, she didn't like women too much, but she did have a few women friends. She loved dirty jokes; she did that with Father Pete: she cursed like sailor and she had that smoker's voice. She was a big woman.

She was full of advice, too. I remember once I was telling her that I was comping some celebrity and she said, "I beg you. You can't comp them. You gotta teach them." I've learned so much from her.

One Sunday night, it was a dead night and a group of about four people came in dressed in black tie. The woman was with CNN, I think, and her husband was a big-time lawyer.

"We just got back. We did our mother's eightieth birthday at 21."

Well, that's all she needed to hear—that they ate somewhere else. She said, "Sit down and eat." They were scared at this point and they did what they were told.

She ordered a filet mignon and a couple of bottles of Veuve Clicquot. She said, "Here, have some." She put the food on our plates and poured Veuve Clicquot in our glasses, as well. These people had just met us, but she knew they were rich.

"Come on, get another bottle," she told them. We had close to six bottles and they had quite a tab.

When I saw her the next night, she said, "That was fun; I almost got them to get six bottles. You gotta get it from those who have it."

I get her point.

I was there for the election, the Super Bowl, and for 9/11.

On 9/11, you went there for the sense of community. The TV was on, people were a tables, you felt a safety, like your home. It was just a warm feeling. I heard that Louie Garcia was in there, doing some shots. He was the chief fire marshall. She said, "Louie have something to eat," and she took care of him.

Joan Rivers played the Cutting Room for four years and she once said, "Elaine gives you a free drink whenever you're ready to leave." This turned out to be true. Joan stopped going to Elaine's for a while because a close friend of hers who went there frequently had died. When I told the reason to Elaine, she responded, "Tell her to grow up."

This was part of her business philosophy.

One of my favorite lines of hers was, "Someone's gotta pay the real estate. You gotta get asses in the seats."

People Soup

Tony Hendra

Tony Hendra has been described by The Independent of London *as "one of the most brilliant comic talents of the post-war period" and by the* New York Times *as "legendary." He began his career in Cambridge University Footlights as the comedy partner of Graham Chapman, later of Monty Python, appeared multiple times on the* Ed Sullivan Show, *was one of the original editors of* National Lampoon, *and produced and directed the Lampoon's off-Broadway hit* Lemmings, *which gave John Belushi, Chevy Chase and Christopher Guest their first starring roles.*

In addition to being a bestselling nonfiction author, he is founder and CEO of the online satirical hub TheFinalEdition. com and co-producer of The Final Edition Radio Hour, and as of 2015, he assumed a new role as CCO (Chief Creative Officer) of the newly resurgent National Lampoon brand.

I don't remember exactly when I first went to Elaine's—hey, it was the sixies—but I know it was a consequence of patronizing a splendid Irish bar called Himself on East Eighty-eighth Street. At Himself, I made my first close New York friend, Malachy McCourt, who held

Tony Hendra and Elaine.

Photo credit: Lucy Hendra.

court there with a spectrum of Irish geniuses from Paul O'Dwyer to Richard Harris. Himself was a grand bar—until midnight when you had to eat something to sop up all the booze. True to Irish form, all the place had to offer was an early, unsuccessful version of fusion cuisine: American Grade-A hamburger, cooked by an Irishman to the consistency of an eight-ball, served on an English muffin.

Luckily 'round the corner on Second Avenue was a bar called Elaine's that actually banned hamburgers. It had the same dark, delicious fug as Himself, but also toothsome food, decent wine, tables you could linger at all night—and writers. Back then, I was a modestly successful comedian (my partner and I headlined for a couple years at Julius Monk's Plaza 9), but writing was in my blood. At Elaine's you could hang around the likes of Lewis Lapham, Gay Talese, Bruce Jay Friedman, Jack Richardson, Warren Hinckle, George Plimpton, Sidney Zion, Herb Sargent . . . Writers and/or editors who talked books, and publishing, writers and articles, magazines and newspapers—anything from low gossip to high-flown debate—till sun-up. Eventually you would even get invited to sit at their tables.

I've lost count of the special moments that happened for one reason or another with one set of people or another in the forty or so years I frequented the dark bar with the yellow awning. But a couple stand out . . .

I was returning from a printing plant in Toledo, Ohio at nine o'clock one chilly October night in 1978, carrying a stack of copies fresh off the press, of *Not The New*

York Times. *The Times* was then going through a major
strike and a bunch of us—a very Elaine's bunch: George
Plimpton, Chris Cerf, Rusty Unger (wife of Tom Guinz-
berg), and myself—had decided to publish a parody of
it, written by eminent or notorious New York literati, to
slake the jones of the city's *Times* readers, deprived for
months of their daily fix.

Pushing through the battered doors of Elaine's, I saw
several large tables in the front of the restaurant packed
with my fellow editors and contributors. This was the big
moment: had their wildly funny collective vision actually
come to fruition? Apparently, yes. As copies were passed
round, the front tables exploded with laughter. Soon the
whole place was rocking. Elaine sat in the midst of the
happy mayhem, the candles on the tables glinting off her
glasses, nodding and smiling. It was one of the greatest
nights of my life.

Flash-forward almost thirty years to my eldest son's
sixteenth birthday. My wife and I had brought him to
Elaine's for dinner. Nick was a tall strong kid, a bas-
ketball player whose ambition was to go to a Division
I school on a full ride. (He achieved this goal.) That
night, though, he was sullen because none of the sports
or movie stars we said might be at the bar were not in
attendance. Elaine joined us. She picked up the vibe at
the table and started chatting with Nick. Sports, being
a teen, his school, parents . . . Soon they were chuckling
away together. I realized I'd never seen Elaine talk to
anyone younger than 25 or 30 unless they were a celebrity and she had to. But she and Nick were clicking big

time. Eventually the moment came for him to go to the real party downtown with his teammates and homies. He got up, told Elaine quite warmly (for him) that it was great to meet her, and turned to leave. Wait, she said, and produced a roll of c-notes the size of an office Rolodex from her skirts. She peeled one off and tucked it in his shirt pocket. "Don't listen to them," she said, indicating us. "Have a good time tonight."

I made life-long friendships at Elaine's—Lapham and Plimpton were just two—though it has to be said that there was such a thing as The Elaine's Friend. Someone you only ever met at Elaine's, who greeted you cordially and shared your table—someone who debated with you fiercely, made you laugh like an idiot, and whose favorite bibendum you knew by heart, but with whom you almost never socialized elsewhere. Over the forty years I went to Elaine's, there were scores upon scores of these friends, kindred spirits of unique charm or staggering talent or both, whom I thought of with affection and respect . . . but only partied or commiserated with, in an unprepossessing, book-lined Second Avenue joint with uncomfortable chairs and wobbly tables.

People have accused Elaine's—perhaps because of The Elaine's Friend Syndrome—of superficiality. But I believe there was simply a curious magic to the place that drew me back year after year for decades; I knew there would always be a few of those kindred spirits, heads turning, arms waving me over to join them as I walked through the door. And that was Elaine's doing.

The night I left Himself and walked into Elaine's, I had no idea why I'd been admitted to the far-flung company of people who always got a table and a quick sit-down from the Big Lady herself. But for some reason, I did. Thousands of others did, too—people who were like me: not especially brilliant or beautiful or famous or fabulous. And they probably don't know why they had been admitted either.

I miss Elaine's and Elaine to this day, terribly. But what I miss most of all is her miraculous, mysterious, and never-to-be replicated recipe for people soup.

Who's on First?
(In Elaine's Bathroom)

Richard Johnson

Richard Johnson, a handsome New Yorker, is less than six degrees of pages or separation from the New York Post's *infamous Page Six. Actually, Johnson is Page Six and has been for quite some time. He has seen or heard it all and then some—and then inked it in for the rest of us to wake up to: the zing-a ling a-ling wohza-powza of many a New York/ Hollywood "scandal." Who can resist ripping through a paper with headlines like "Headless Body Found in Topless Bar"? And we're just getting warmed up.*

WE ASKED RICHARD Johnson for a few of his favorite Elaine's memories. Here goes:

The best story ever was the one I wrote on Page Six about the night that Gianni Uzielli's girlfriend was caught in flagrante with Mets star Keith Hernandez.

The two had disappeared after many drinks, and Uzielli finally left the table to look for them. He found her performing fellatio on Hernandez. Then came an operatic scene as the cuckolded Uzielli screamed at the woman, who sobbed.

As a reporter, the big issue for me the next day was determining whether it had happened in the ladies room, as I had been told, or in the men's room, as Hernandez maintained. This issue being, who followed whom? Who instigated this act of betrayal?

I'll also never forget the night George Plimpton and I debated the JFK assassination and the Warren Commission report. Plimpton believed in the single gunman and the magic bullet. I was and remain convinced Lee Harvey Oswald was set up by co-conspirators.

Then there was the night Bo Dietl and I got into a discussion of Donald Manes's suicide in 1986. Dietl said, "What a coward. What kind of man leaves his family like that?"

I remarked that he didn't take the easy way out with pills or carbon monoxide.

He stabbed himself in the heart with a kitchen knife. That isn't easy.

Good times.

"I Would Not Be the Person I Am Today if I Had Not Gone Into Elaine's."

Libby Schoettle

Elizabeth Schoettle (who often goes by Libby) is a New York City–based mixed/media collage artist who uses Polaroids as well as found photographs. Libby collects images of women, and girls, specifically in search of ones who bear resemblance to her body (and her mood) as a way to identify with how she is feeling. Libby had her first solo mixed-media art show at Meredith Ward Fine Art NY in 2007 and is currently working on her first memoir-based novel "revealing" her life as an artist. As well, she is the subject of a feature documentary film, directed by filmmaker Jyll Johnstone, about her life as this artist. Libby lives and works in New York City.

WHEN I FIRST moved to New York, I lived above a restaurant, where I met Gianni Uzielli (former owner of Uzi's restaurant). We responded to each other in a very past-life kind of way; we were instant friends. I was about twenty-two, it was around 1996. He was probably in is fifties.

Gianni took me to Elaine's.

It was a very powerful experience, going there was an immediate connection for me in terms of the energy and ambiance; I thought, "This is New York."

There are so many places in New York and Elaine's did not exist anywhere else. Sitting in a front table at Elaine's was not something very common; I just took it for granted. People would look at you, like, who is this person sitting at a door table? I liked the show-star atmosphere and there were all sorts of types in there; you felt like you wanted to be them or know them.

It was a tough ambiance to recreate. Now people are depressed. There's no club like Elaine's to go into. It was a very mature, comfortable atmosphere and you felt like you belonged there.

I didn't understand Elaine when I first met her, but she had a serious personality and I liked it. I had never met a woman like that. I would see the way she was with her restaurant, the way she managed it, the way she looked around, and which people she let in and which ones she didn't. She was like a man. She didn't back down and she really owned it. I really respected it and really enjoyed her presence. There was something really strong about her.

Everyone liked her or they didn't like her. There was no in-between. I went to Elaine's over a period of fourteen years. At first, she made comments, like, "What's she doing here?" It never bothered me because she was so blatant, so honest.

I got to know her as best as I could. We got to a point where she said. "Let's go shopping. I'll pick you up and we'll go fabric shopping." I loved her style for what she was. She was big and she pulled off her clothing so well, and she wanted to take me to her dressmaker. It never happened. I felt kind of important. I mean, we're talking about shopping.

I loved the ladies' room, the posters. You could feel the energy of the dead people who moved on. There was something poetic and romantic about that.

I went to the party Elaine's after Gianni's funeral. I found it very sad. (N.B. Elaine and Gianni had a falling out when he was opening a new restaurant. She felt that he was deliberately taking customers away from her, and their friendship ruptured.)

I felt the emotion between them and they were really close. I felt that when he left, she was never the same. I really felt like she missed him. He was an incredible spark in her life. He was so funny and there was no one like him. There was no one like either of them; their banter was wonderful. They were both very stubborn people. They both thought they were always right. Theirs was a serious falling out. I really felt like she missed him, but couldn't let him back in.

Everywhere I went with Gianni, everyone knew him. I thought it was absolutely miraculous . . . I would not be the person I am today if I had not gone into Elaine's with him. It made me aware of what my taste is. I was so fresh to New York. It was magical to me. It was a perfect match when I walked in there.

Afterword

"What really knocks me out is a book that, when you're all done reading it, you wish the author that wrote it was a terrific friend of yours and you could call him up on the phone whenever you felt like it. That doesn't happen much, though."

—J.D. Salinger, *The Catcher in the Rye*

To MANY OF her friends and onlookers, Elaine Kaufman was the author, without the title, that they wanted to know.

Her language wasn't always the King's English: she was often "short, but not so sweet;" funny, irascible, New York sarcastic, observant, abusive and better informed than most newscasters and journalists.

She sat down to enjoy life with her favorite authors, politicians, artists, journalists: those she considered family.

At times she shared their food, without asking, and billed them for it. No one seemed to mind. It often seemed like the thing to do to criticize Elaine's food. Perhaps that was because that there little else to criticize if you were nestled or ruffled in her ample nest, and longed to stay there.

Elaine's was different. Elaine felt comfortable, moving from table to table, and making room at tables for those who were on their own. Some of us have had that opportunity, others never will.

So many of her friends miss her deeply and know that Elaine and Elaine's shall never be replaced. She leaves behind writers, photographers, and other aspiring souls whose lives she has scrupulously sculpted. Their knowledge, anecdotes, skills, and introductions are welcomed by the next generation.

So long, Elaine.

Your legend lives on in books, both dog-eared and yet to be written.